GOD'S
Portrait
OF A BEAUTIFUL WOMAN

DOROTHY DAVIS

REGULAR BAPTIST PRESS
1300 North Meacham Road
Schaumburg, Illinois 60173-4806

GOD'S PORTRAIT OF A BEAUTIFUL WOMAN
© 2006 Regular Baptist Press • Schaumburg, Illinois
All rights reserved • Printed in U.S.A.
www.RegularBaptistPress.org • 1-800-727-4440
RBP5228 • ISBN 978-0-87227-186-9

Sixth printing—2010

Contents

In Dedication

To my husband, Dale, and our children—Paul, Kristen, Kevin, and Seth—who have supported me by their love, patience, encouragement, and prayers as the Lord has worked on my portrait.

Preface

Have you gone to a museum and looked at the painted portrait of some prestigious person of long ago? Did you marvel at the ability of the painter's hand to capture the character and particular beauty of that human being?

Since the first moment of creation, God has been the Master Painter. We often acknowledge this when we see a sunset, the ocean, or the brilliance of an autumn hillside. But as the Master Painter, God also desires to paint portraits. Each person, whom He has created, has the potential to be a portrait of godly beauty and the fulfillment of His perfect design for that human being.

Psalm 139:13 refers to the fact that God created our "inmost being" ("reins") and put us together in our mothers' wombs. Not only that; verse 16 says that God knows all the days that are ordained for us. From these verses we learn that God is not some distant spectator of our lives but the very One Who designed us, made us, and planned all our days. At this very moment He is at work in His children's lives, making each of us what He intended us to be. "For it is God which worketh in you both to will and to do of his good pleasure" (Philippians 2:13).

A painter starts with a canvas and a palette of colors that are applied with a brush or other tool for the desired result. Think of your life as a canvas upon which the Lord is painting a portrait that will conform to the perfect design of His will for you. The purpose of this study is to help you cooperate with His work in your life as He seeks to make you into His masterpiece. He desires to make you into a beautiful portrait of His grace—more beautiful and more captivating than any portrait that has been painted by man!

How to Use This Study

Each lesson in this study is divided into five sections. Follow these suggestions as you prepare each lesson.

I: VERSE(S) FOR MEMORIZATION AND MEDITATION

Memorize the verse or verses. Or, at least read them several times in preparation for the lesson. Answer the questions that pertain to the verse(s).

II: EVALUATION FOR PREPARATION

The questions in this section are designed to prepare your heart to receive God's Word. These questions will not be discussed in your Bible study group.

III: SCRIPTURES FOR STUDY

The questions in this section are aimed at concentrating on the actual text of God's Word and understanding what it says. Answer the questions as completely as you can. Use a standard dictionary to look up any words you do not know.

IV: APPLICATION FOR GROWTH

As you answer the questions in this section, you will see how the truths of God's Word apply to your life.

V: CHALLENGE FOR CHANGE

The suggestions in this section will help you put into practice the things you have learned. As with section II, these questions will not be discussed in the group.

Preparing the Canvas: The Proper Support

OF PRIMARY IMPORTANCE in any great and enduring painting is the preparation of the canvas. As anxious as the artist may be to apply his mastery in color and texture, he knows that if the canvas lacks proper support and surface preparation, the result will be a waste of his best efforts. The condition of the canvas itself is as essential to a great work of art as what goes on it.

We may make a parallel to this in our own lives. Each of us is like a piece of canvas with the potential to become God's "work of art." But in order to be receptive to God's masterful working in our lives, we must have the proper "support" and "preparation." The first two lessons of this study deal with the necessary conditions in order for us to be receptive to God's work upon our hearts.

I: VERSES FOR MEMORIZATION AND MEDITATION

"My sheep hear my voice, and I know them, and they follow me: And I give unto them eternal life; and they shall never perish, neither shall any man pluck them out of my hand" (John 10:27, 28).

Earlier in John 10, Jesus said some people were not His sheep (v. 26). There are only two groups of people: His sheep and not His sheep.

1. In John 10:27 and 28 what did Jesus say about His relationship with His sheep? *He*

2. How do His sheep respond to Him?

When they hear His voice, they follow Him.

II: EVALUATION FOR PREPARATION

Think about the following questions; then jot down your answers in a few sentences.

1. Have you ever personally received God's gift of eternal life? How do you know?

2. Do you think you could ever lose your place in Heaven? Why? *No*

John 5:24
Jn. 14:1-6

III: SCRIPTURES FOR STUDY

Just as the first step in preparing to paint a portrait is to put proper support under the canvas, so, too, God can begin to paint His masterpiece in us only if our lives have been properly placed upon the "support" of His Son, Jesus Christ. Apart from Him we are unable to please God or be conformed by Him to His divine design.

How does a person obtain this support? It is called "salvation." Think of it in terms of a four-sided framework.

Side 1: The Bible states that every person is a sinner, separated from a holy God. No one can enter Heaven because of his/her sins. A person must acknowledge her sinful condition.

1. Romans 3:9 says that everyone—Jew or Gentile—is _under_ _sin_.

2. Romans 3:23 states, "For _all_ _have_ _sinned_ . . . ."

3. Ephesians 2:1 describes us as " _dead_ in _transgressions_ and _sin_ ."

4. Why is it so important to acknowledge our sinfulness?

Side 2: The Bible states that the end result of sin is eternal death (separation from God in Hell). We are unable to do anything to rectify our sinful condition. But because God loves us and does not want us to spend eternity in Hell, He punished His sinless Son, Jesus, upon the cross for our sins. Salvation is not a result of anything we can do, but it is a free gift from God, based on what Christ has already done for us on the cross.

5. According to Romans 5:6, for what kind of people did Jesus die?
ungodly

6. Romans 5:8 restates that idea. God showed His love in that Jesus died for us _while_ _we_ _were_ _still_ _sinners_ .

7. First Corinthians 15:3 says that Christ died for _our_ _sins_ .

8. Titus 3:4 and 5 teach us that God saved us according to His _mercy_ . That means He withholds the punishment we rightly deserve because the Lord Jesus took it for us.

Side 3: The Bible teaches that we may obtain forgiveness of sins and eternal life in Heaven by coming to God in faith and by believing that Christ died for our sins, putting our trust totally in Him to save us.

9. Read John 6:37 and 40. What two things did Jesus say we must do?

repent and believe

10. What has He promised to do in return?

raise us up and give salvation

11. Can you think of some other verses that explain how we can receive God's gift of salvation? If you need help, look up the words "believe" and "receive" in a Bible concordance.

Roman 3.

Side 4: Salvation is not a feeling, but a decision. Romans 10:9 and 10 say we are to confess with our mouths and believe in our hearts that these things are so (i.e., we are sinners, we cannot save ourselves, Jesus died for us).

12. Once we have made this decision, what is God's promise in Romans 10:13? *Everyone who calls on the name of the Lord will be saved.*

This is the framework of salvation. If you have placed your life upon this support, it will not fail or fall apart. You don't have to worry that it will become loose or wobbly or that it will break apart. As believers in Christ and recipients of God's salvation, we have "eternal security." We can never lose our place in Heaven because we do not get or keep ourselves saved—Christ is the One Who has done the work by shedding His blood.

13. How do the following verses give us this assurance?

John 3:16   *If we believe in Him we will not perish*

John 10:27-29

never be plucked from His hand

1 John 5:11-13

that we may KNOW

Jude 24

We will be with God

14. Review the four basic truths of salvation by completing each side of the frame.

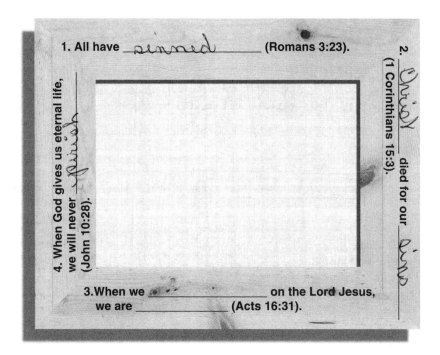

1. All have *sinned* (Romans 3:23).

2. *Christ* died for our *sins* (1 Corinthians 15:3).

3. When we *believe* on the Lord Jesus, we are *saved* (Acts 16:31).

4. When God gives us eternal life, we will never *perish* (John 10:28).

IV: APPLICATION FOR GROWTH

1. You may have been saved for a long time or just a short time, but the wonder of God's gracious provision should always be with you. Think about each of the following topics; write a sentence about how each one affects your life.

Forgiveness

Those things I did in the past are gone.

God's love

I enjoy the peace and joy of knowing He loves me!

Jesus Christ

He is Savior of my life, my salvation,

Salvation

I am His child!

Eternal security

I will be with the LORD forever

2. Select one of those topics and describe further how it will help make a portrait of beauty out of your life.

V: CHALLENGE FOR CHANGE

Select at least one challenge to put into practice this week.

1. Look back at the statements you wrote in section II. Answer the questions again. If you know for certain that you have received Jesus Christ as your personal Savior from sin, thank God for saving you. Ask Him to change your life according to His will as you study these lessons.

2. If you have not made this all-important decision in your life, won't you reconsider the verses presented in this lesson and call upon God to save you? Remember: Only with this "support" can God begin to paint His portrait of beauty in you.

FINISHING TOUCHES

IN PREPARATION for the studies to follow, you need to evaluate the condition of your portrait. Are you living securely in the forgiveness, love, and power of the Lord Jesus Christ? Or does it seem to you that your life has fallen apart as the result of events, relationships, and choices? If you are dissatisfied with your life, let Christ Jesus give you the stability that only He can give. Place your trust in Him today—for life right now and for eternity. Having done this, you can watch with excitement as He works on the portrait of your life in His own special way.

Preparing the Canvas: Stretching and Priming

ONCE THE ARTIST puts the canvas on a support, he could begin to paint the portrait, but the finished piece would be flawed and fragile. The canvas must undergo two more procedures before it is completely ready to receive the artist's work.

First of all, the artist must be certain that the canvas has been tightly stretched in all directions upon the framework. This will allow the canvas to display his finished work without bulging or warping, which could crack the dried paints and ruin his work. Stretching the canvas produces the proper surface to best display the artist's design and skill.

Second, the surface of the canvas must be primed. Usually a type of gesso is used. Gesso is a white, glue-like substance that causes the paints to adhere when they are applied. This gives the portrait a great enduring quality; the artist's work will not fade as time goes on.

In the portrait of a woman's life, two conditions are necessary to assure that the Lord's work will take hold and endure. As a believer, she must acknowledge the sovereign purposes of God in all her life's circumstances and the right of Jesus Christ to be the Lord of her life. Just as stretching the canvas makes it the ideal surface for "showing off" the artist's work, so the circumstances that God allows in our lives will help us display "God-like-ness" (godliness). Similarly, as priming the canvas makes it receptive and adhesive, so the decision that we make to let Christ be the Lord of our lives makes us receive and hold on to God's work in us as He convicts, teaches, and changes us.

If you and I will receive all the hard circumstances of life and grow in them, and if we will allow Jesus Christ to be not only our Savior but also Lord in all areas of our lives, then the portrait that God unveils "in that day" (2 Thessalonians 1:10) will be astounding in its beauty and grace—a glorious reflection of HIM! Let's look into His Word and encourage our hearts to be stretched and primed!

I: VERSES FOR MEMORIZATION AND MEDITATION

"As ye have therefore received Christ Jesus the Lord, so walk ye in him: Rooted and built up in him, and stablished in the faith, as ye have been taught, abounding therein with thanksgiving" (Colossians 2:6, 7).

1. According to these verses, how are we to receive Christ Jesus?

to walk with Him in faith & thanksgiving receive and hold on to Gods work in us

2. Look up the word "lord" in a dictionary or Bible dictionary. What does it say?

master
British" nobleman
God
Jesus Christ

II: EVALUATION FOR PREPARATION

1. What are some of the hard circumstances (past or present) that have been part of your life?

infidelity / death of loved ones / seperation from family dependence on others

2. How have you reacted to these things?

hurt, anger, acceptance

3. What changes have you made in your life since becoming a Christian?

More forgiving

III: SCRIPTURES FOR STUDY

1. Look up the following verses and jot down in your own words what each verse teaches about God's role as Planner and Creator.

Psalm 119:73 *God made me & has a plan for my life*

Psalm 139:15, 16
He knew me before I was even born & knew all my life & how long I will live

Exodus 4:10, 11
He knows all our strengths & weaknesses & will supply our needs

Proverbs 16:9
Even as we make plans, He determines our path

Proverbs 16:4
Everything is according to His plan

Romans 8:28, 29
Because we belong to Him — he will work all things to bring about His will for His glory in our lives

2. Write a brief paragraph that summarizes how these verses relate to your life.
Nothing will happen in my life that God doesn't allow & He will allow nothing outside His will

I Cor. 10:13

3. Look up the following verses that speak of the tests and trials of life. Fill in answers under each column.

Verse	Words used to describe "trial"	Result of trial	Additional comments
Job 23:10	tested	refinement	
Psalm 119:67	afflicted	obedience	
Romans 5:3	suffering	perseverance	we grow in faith
2 Corinthians 4:17	troubles	eternal glory	
Hebrews 12:11	discipline	righteousness & peace	trained by our trials
1 Peter 1:6, 7	grief	improved faith	a closer walk with Him

4. Based on these verses, how should we respond to suffering? What will be the beneficial results? Look upon them as a teaching experience to gain strength in God along with closeness in Him

5. When a saved woman allows Jesus Christ to be the Lord of her life as well as her Savior, how is this revealed in her life? Read Luke 6:46-49; Colossians 2:6, 7; Ephesians 5:8-17; 1 Peter 3:13-16.

He is the foundation of her life. He is the one she turns to for guidance & direction - the source of her strength & comfort

IV: APPLICATION FOR GROWTH

1. Consider again the difficult aspects of your life (including race, religious upbringing, handicaps, illnesses, accidents, death of loved ones, birth order, scars, abuse, divorce, etc.). What beneficial results has God worked for your good through these difficulties?

Dependence on HIM!

2. How should you respond to trials in the future?

Use them to gain strength in your relationship with the Lord

3. What attitudes may keep you from making Christ your Lord?

pride, self-sufficancy -

4. What attitudes do you need in order to be receptive to God's work in you?   *willing to serve Him, humility caring, loving*

5. What things make it difficult to make Jesus Christ the Lord of your life?   *Sinful nature*

V: CHALLENGE FOR CHANGE

Select at least one challenge to put into practice this week.

1. Make a list of five hard circumstances in your life and the corresponding benefits. Thank God for these things.

2. Do you have a prayer partner to support you as you strive to make your life a "living sacrifice" to the Lord? Ask someone to pray for you that, as you face the trials and obstacles of life, you will respond to them according to God's will for you.

3. Has the Lord shown you a specific area in which you have resisted His Lordship? a decision? a habit? an attitude? a relationship? Commit yourself to do what He says as you talk to Him in prayer. Think of a practical way to help yourself make this change a reality; e.g., memorize a verse; tell a godly friend of your commitment and ask her to pray for you or help you by some other means.

FINISHING TOUCHES

APART FROM SALVATION, the two conditions we have studied in this lesson are foundational to our relationship with God. Our response to God's working through our circumstances and our obedience to Christ's commands will determine how enduring and effective our walk with the Lord will be. (See Luke 8:5-15 for the way in which trials and self-centeredness will choke God's Word and work in a life.) Being "stretched" by our circumstances is not easy. Being "primed"—having one's self covered over and hidden by the Lord Jesus—takes humility. But stretching and priming will result in a portrait of excellence. As women of God, we should desire nothing less.

Are you being stretched by life's circumstances? See it as God's way of making you into His portrait of a beautiful woman. Is your life being covered over by the likeness of Jesus Christ? Is He the Lord of your thoughts, attitudes, words, and actions? Ultimately, God's will is for your portrait to be a portrait of Him.

Putting on the Paint

T HE ARTIST STANDS ready in his studio. On his right hand is his table
with his supplies and paints. On his left hand is a white canvas on
an easel. How will he get the colors on the canvas? By what
means will he apply his design? How will he produce his portrait of
beauty?

The artist looks to his table. He selects a certain brush, puts it to the
palette and begins to lay upon the canvas the shapes and colors of his
plan and purpose. Suppose for a moment that someone crept in and
snatched away the canvas. Or what if the lights went out, leaving the
canvas in muddled darkness? How could the artist carry out his work? His
brushes, no matter how excellent or valuable, would be unable to carry
out their task.

The Master Painter, in His omniscient design, has put the Person of
the Holy Spirit and His eternal Word upon our hearts to carry out His
plan and purpose for each of His children. They are poised and ready to
do the work He desires them to do. How often, though, does the enemy
of our souls, the Devil, come in to snatch away the conviction and
leading of God's Spirit and the Word from our hearts? How frequently is
the "light" of God's grace snuffed out by worldliness and sin so that we
quench His Spirit and resist His Word? How then can the Master apply
the colors of godliness to our lives when we hinder the work of the Spirit
and the Word?

We must learn not to hinder them! We must practice locking the
doors of our hearts so that the Devil cannot influence us! As we "walk in
the light" (1 John 1:7), God's Word will keep shining into the dark places
of our hearts. Our excitement will mount as we anticipate what the
Master's hand will accomplish as we let Him freely do His work.

I. VERSES FOR MEMORIZATION AND MEDITATION

"Thy testimonies are wonderful: therefore doth my soul keep them. The entrance of thy words giveth light; it giveth understanding unto the simple" (Psalm 119:129, 130).

1. How do these verses describe God's Word?

wonderful

2. What benefits of God's Word did the psalmist name?

give light / give understanding

3. What was the response of the psalmist to God's Word?

my soul keeps them

II: EVALUATION FOR PREPARATION

Underline the best answer to each statement.

1. I read/study God's Word daily.

    Never   Occasionally   (Usually)

2. I spend time praying and confessing my sins daily.

    Never   Occasionally   (Usually)

3. I go to Sunday School and church to worship God and hear His Word.

    Never   Occasionally   (Usually)

4. I try to memorize and think about verses from the Bible.

Never   Occasionally   (Usually)

5. I pray daily for the filling and guiding of the Holy Spirit in my life.

Never   Occasionally   (Usually)

III: SCRIPTURES FOR STUDY

1. Read John 14:16, 17, and 26. Where does God's Spirit dwell?

within us

2. According to Jesus, how does the Spirit help believers?

will teach us all things & counsel us

In the letter to the Galatians, Paul said that it is futile to try to live a holy life by our own efforts. We can't do that because of the "flesh," the sin principle with which we struggle daily. Answer the following questions after you read Galatians 5:16-26.

3. What two parties are locked in conflict within us?

Our sinful nature
The Holy Spirit

4. According to verses 16 and 25, how are we to live ("walk")?

by the Holy Spirit

5. What do you think this means?

Put away our sinful nature

6. What will happen as a result?

A closer walk with the Lord

7. What happens when we allow the flesh to take control?

we turn away from God

8. What are some qualities the Spirit is seeking to develop in us?

love, joy, peace, patience, kindness, goodness, faithfulness, gentleness, selfcontrol,

9. According to verses 24 and 25, how can a Christian overcome fleshly desires? (Also read Romans 6:6, 7, and 11.)

live by the Spirit & keep in step with the Spirit

10. If the Spirit of God were not within us, what would happen?

The sinful nature would take control

Read Ephesians 4:30 and 1 Thessalonians 5:19.

11. What do these two verses instruct us NOT to do?

Do not grieve the Holy Spirit

12. In what ways do we hinder the work of the Spirit in our lives?

Rage, Anger, bitterness, unwholesome talk

13. Who has the responsibility NOT to do these two things?

Me

Read 2 Timothy 3:16 and 17.

14. Who is the source of all Scripture (the Old and New Testaments)?

God

15. For what are the Scriptures helpful? Write a brief definition of each word.

teaching
rebuking
correcting
training

16. Write in your own words why God gave us the Scriptures.

So we can be competant to do the work He gave us to do

17. Read Psalm 119:47 and Jeremiah 15:16. What should be our attitude toward God's Word?   Love, joy & praise

18. List four things we ought to do with the Word.

Acts 17:11   examine carefully

Psalm 119:11   hide in our heart

Psalm 119:97   meditate on it

James 1:22

dont just listen to it do what it says !

IV: APPLICATION FOR GROWTH

1. Reconsider the Galatians 5 passage. (a) What activities are necessary to keep in step with the Spirit?

loving, joy, kindness, forgiveness be gentle, peaceful, self control

(b) How will this promote God's work in your life?

a closer relationship with Him

2. Based on the verses you studied about the Scriptures, list several reasons why God has given us His Word.

To show Himself to us A closer walk with Him

3. When a woman puts a high priority on reading, memorizing, and thinking about God's Word, what will be the results in her life?

Inner peace

4. In what ways do you think Satan will try to hinder you daily from keeping in step with the Spirit and spending time in God's Word?

Busyness,

V: CHALLENGE FOR CHANGE

Select at least one challenge to put into practice this week.

1. Based on the Galatians 5 passage, ask yourself the following questions:

In my own life, do I see more of the acts of the flesh or the fruit of the Spirit? Am I regularly doing those things that are necessary to keep step with the Spirit?

If the flesh is more in control, recommit yourself to stop grieving and quenching the Spirit. Ask the Lord to forgive you. Thank God each day for the ministry of the Spirit within you. Establish the habit of daily prayer and confession. Become involved in a Bible-believing, Bible-preaching church. Get untangled from sinful practices, relationships, and attitudes, and replace them with spiritually healthy ones. Find a godly person to help and encourage you.

2. What is your attitude toward God's precious Word? The psalmist declared that he would not forget or neglect God's Word (Psalm 119:16, 61). Do you read and search the Word daily? Try a read-through-the-Bible schedule or a Bible with daily portions outlined. Are you memorizing verses and thinking about them? Write verses on 3" x 5" cards and post them where you will see them often to memorize and think on them. Find someone with whom you can memorize and do it as a team. Ask the Lord for His help to do this. All Christians need God's enabling to read and understand His Word (Psalm 119:73, 125). Remember, it's His Word, and He has given it to you. His will is for you to be helped by it. If you have been neglecting it, confess this to Him and begin today to delight in God's Word.

FINISHING TOUCHES

THE ENEMY OF GOD (and man) has many tactics to keep a portrait of God's from becoming a finished, radiant masterpiece. He will try to snatch away the life-changing power of the Spirit and the light of God's Word, thus rendering us powerless to grow in godliness. We must by God's power and grace, through faith and prayer, resist his schemes (Ephesians 6:10-18).

Several verses speak of the Bible in terms of light in our lives (Psalms 19:8; 119:105, 130). To remove the light of God's Word from our lives puts us in a state of spiritual dusk from day to day. To grieve and quench the Holy Spirit is to put out our spiritual fire.

The Lord wants to work upon the portraits of our lives. He wants us to reflect His glory. The Word brings knowledge of His glory. The Spirit transforms us into His glory. "But we all, with open face beholding as in a glass the glory of the Lord, are changed into the same image from glory to glory, even as by the Spirit of the Lord" (2 Corinthians 3:18).

We must make ourselves accessible to the Spirit's leading and the Word's enlightening. Through the work of both, we can become portraits of His glory.

L E S S O N 4

Shaped by Our Thoughts

I MAGINE YOUR LIFE as a painting, hanging on a vast wall of a museum. People wander about, stopping to consider each work of art. What do they see when they stop in front of the painting of your life? Serenity? confusion? sharpness? soft, soothing shapes? vibrant color? muddied, muted tones? When we grab the brush from the Master's hand and attempt to paint a self-portrait, we end up with quite a mess. But as we let Him do the work, He will clarify the colors and smooth out the lines.

God's portrait of a beautiful woman begins with our thoughts. What we allow ourselves to think about will shape the outlines of the painting of our lives. These shapes, in turn, will be colored by our attitudes, our words, and our behavior.

To use another illustration, think of thoughts as seeds. The plants that take root and grow from these seeds are attitudes. The blossoms or thorns the plants produce are words and actions. Can you see the necessity of planting the proper seeds in the soil of your mind? Have you been planting seeds for weeds? As we study God's Word, He will give us insight into the kind of thoughts that are pleasing to Him.

I: VERSE FOR MEMORIZATION AND MEDITATION

"For they that are after the flesh do mind the things of the flesh; but they that are after the Spirit, the things of the Spirit" (Romans 8:5).

1. Describe the thought-life of a person who is controlled by her flesh. selfishness, bitterness, anger

2. Describe the thought-life of one who is walking with the Spirit.

Compassion, forgiveness, wanting to please God.

II: EVALUATION FOR PREPARATION

1. Where is your mind: on the desires of the flesh or the desires of the Holy Spirit?

2. What kind of thoughts contribute to this mind-set?

listening to God's Word

III: SCRIPTURES FOR STUDY

1. Look up the following verses and jot down what they teach about our thoughts: Psalm 7:9; Psalm 26:2; Jeremiah 17:10; Revelation 2:23. (The word "heart" refers to man's innermost being and includes, among other things, his thoughts. Several verses in this lesson and the following one refer to the heart since it relates both to thoughts and attitudes.)

God searches & knows our thoughts. He examines our heart & mind. He rewards us according to conduct & deeds

2. What kind of thoughts occupy the mind of a person who rejects the knowledge of God and is dominated by sin?
Matthew 15:16-20

Evil, destructive thoughts

Romans 1:28-31

greed, depravity, gossip, strife envy, disobedience

Philippians 3:18, 19

they are enemies of the cross their destiny is destruction

3. By contrast, what are some things God wants His children to think about?

1 Samuel 12:24 *Fear the Lord & serve Him with your whole heart*

Psalm 63:6 *Think on Him all through the night*

Psalm 77:11, 12 *remember His deeds and meditate on them*

Psalm 107:43 *Consider the great love of the Lord*

Psalm 119:15, 99, 148

meditate on Him

Philippians 4:8 *let your thoughts be on all things true, noble, lovely, admirable, right, pure, excellant or praiseworthy*

Hebrews 3:1 *fix your thoughts on Jesus*

Hebrews 10:24 *how we can encourage one another*

4. How can we have a Spirit-controlled mind? Jot down what each of these verses teaches.

Romans 12:2 Do not conform to the world but be transformed in your mind

Colossians 3:16 Let Christ's words dwell in us & love one another with gratitude in our hearts

Hebrews 4:12 The Word of God penetrates and judges thoughts and attitude

Psalm 119:11 Hide God's Word in our hearts that we might not sin against Him

Joshua 1:8 Meditate on the Word day & night

2 Corinthians 10:5 Take captive every thought and make it obedient to Christ

Philippians 4:6, 7 Be anxious for nothing. Take everything to God in prayer and He will give peace & guard our hearts

Hebrews 4:16 Approach the throne of grace with confidence that we may receive mercy and grace

5. What characterizes the life of a person whose mind is controlled by the Spirit and filled with spiritual thoughts?

Isaiah 26:3 *Peace*

Romans 8:6 *Peace*

Philippians 4:6, 7 *Peace*

6. What additional insights about the mind do you find in these verses?

Matthew 22:37 *Love the LORD with all your heart and mind*

1 Corinthians 2:14-16 *With the mind of Christ, He can instruct us.*

IV: APPLICATION FOR GROWTH

1. The Bible teaches that God judges a Christian's thoughts. (See section III-1.) Do you think Christians realize this? How should this knowledge challenge us? *Not always - to let our thoughts be His thoughts*

2. Does the flesh still plague your thought-life? (See section III-2.) Why might this be?

Not walking as closely as we should with Jesus

3. What "thought exercises" described in section III-3 do you need to do more regularly?

be more concerned for others

4. Which of the verses listed in section III-4 challenges you to become a woman whose thoughts are more Spirit-controlled?

5. (a) Why do you think the quality of peace is associated with a Spirit-controlled mind?

If you are allowing the Spirit to control your thoughts there are very few doubts

(b) How is peace destroyed by a sin-filled mind?

You can't have peace without peaceful thoughts

6. How, then, is the portrait of your life affected by your thoughts?

Your thoughts control your actions

V: CHALLENGE FOR CHANGE

Select at least one challenge to put into practice this week.

1. Choose a verse to memorize and meditate upon that relates to the thought-life. If you have a problem in a particular area (e.g., worry, impurity, faultfinding), find a verse that will help you deal with this area. Find a verse in this lesson or a Bible concordance. Ask the Lord to help you make these thoughts captive and obedient to Christ (2 Corinthians 10:5).

2. Take a "mental purity" inventory. What practices/habits/activities are reinforcing wrong thoughts? Are you feeding your thought-life with wrong reading materials, TV programs that make sin seem acceptable, music, fantasizing? Determine to "put off the old man [flesh] with his deeds" (Colossians 3:9). Remember that Satan will make every effort to keep your mind away from spiritual things, so resist him with practices that will encourage godliness; e.g., reading God's Word and spiritually helpful books; listening to or singing good Christian music. Go boldly before God's throne and seek His help; spend time in the Word and in prayer.

3. When you find your life lacking peace, examine your thoughts to see where you have allowed Satan to gain a foothold in your mind. Give that area back to God and strengthen your mind with Scripture and prayer.

FINISHING TOUCHES

YOUR MIND IS a battleground. If God's enemy can gain control, what havoc he can cause in your spiritual life! Confusion, discontentment, bitterness, envy, impurity, discouragement, despair, rebellion, materialism, worry—the list goes on and on! The description of the Spirit-controlled mind is short and sweet: life and peace (Romans 8:6). The person whose mind is grounded in the truth of God can truly live in the *now*. She can deal with reality by the power and grace of God. The woman who is listening to Satan's lies is living in an "if only" world and is Satan's spiritual hostage.

Is the Spirit of God able to shape the portrait of your life with life and peace? Or has Satan caused your life to look like one of those abstract paintings in which every part is twisted out of its proper place? You are being shaped by your thoughts. What kind of shape are you in?

The Tint of Attitudes

A S THE ARTIST begins to work, he stands before a white canvas, the ideal background for allowing each color put upon it to be reflected in its full purity and richness. However, the artist may choose to put a "wash" over the face of the canvas—a thin, transparent tint of color that will cast a certain tone upon the finished painting. As a result, each color that is put upon the canvas will be subtly shaded by the "wash" rather than showing forth its true purity and brilliance.

The canvas of our lives ought to be white with Christlike attitudes. In this way, as the Master applies the various colors to our lives, each one will reflect purity and spiritual beauty. However, if we have allowed the canvas of our lives to be tinted by ungodly attitudes (which develop as a result of continued ungodly thoughts), this will cast a shade over all the other aspects of our portraits.

What exactly are attitudes? The concept is rather nebulous. We would all admit to having attitudes toward people, ideas, practices, circumstances, events. But many times we aren't even aware that we have certain attitudes, not to mention knowing what they are. Attitudes are real and influential; they proceed from our inmost being.

The dictionary defines "attitude" as both a mental position with regard to a fact or state and a feeling or emotion toward a fact or state. So attitudes involve both the mind and emotions. We have already noted that the word "heart" in God's Word means the wellspring of our thoughts and attitudes, which are closely related.

Has your canvas been tinted by your attitudes? When your finished portrait is revealed, will you find that the colors of your life have been tainted by a dark, sullied stain or a harsh, glaring tone? Even now, your attitudes are casting their effects upon your life—revealing themselves in your words, deeds, and even your appearance. Let's keep the canvas white by allowing the work of God's Word and Spirit upon our ungodly attitudes.

I: VERSES FOR MEMORIZATION AND MEDITATION

"Put off concerning the former conversation [manner of life] the old man, which is corrupt according to the deceitful lusts; And be renewed in the spirit of your mind; And that ye put on the new man, which after God is created in righteousness and true holiness" (Ephesians 4:22–24).

1. Describe what is meant by "the old man."

   the person, thoughts and attitudes we were before Christ became our Saviour

2. What characterizes "the new man"?

   the more Christ-like person we become after giving our hearts to Him

3. What are we commanded to do in these verses?

   Become more like Him

II: EVALUATION FOR PREPARATION

Do you have ungodly attitudes you need to put off? If so, what are they? *irritation*

III: SCRIPTURES FOR STUDY

1. Several Bible characters displayed God-fearing, humble attitudes in situations where they could have been resentful, stubborn, or self-

centered. Look up each reference, identify the godly character, his/her attitude, and the outcome.

Genesis 13:1-17

Abram, attitude of compassion, love & caring. God gave Abram all the land he could see and blessed him and his offspring

Genesis 45:1-15

Joseph, forgiveness, he was reunited with his family & greatly blessed.

1 Samuel 24:1-15

David, in a position to kill Saul but didn't, He recieved God's favor

1 Samuel 25:2-35

David, peaceful, patient — forgiveness and less bloodshed

Acts 15:36-41

Paul, disagreement with Barnabas they seperated & Paul strengthened the churches in Syria and Cilicia

2. Read Philippians 2:5-11. What attitudes of Christ are described in this passage? *servant, humble*

3. Each of the following references presents a situation where the Lord Jesus manifested the attitudes Paul wrote about in Philippians 2. Briefly describe the setting and the attitude(s) displayed.

Luke 5:12, 13

humbleness, mercy

Luke 19:1-10

forgiveness, repentance

Mark 10:13-16

love, tenderness

John 8:1-11

judgment, unforgiveness / mercy & grace

John 13:4, 5

humbleness, servitude = LOVE

4. Read Romans 12:1-3 and 9-21. As we present ourselves as "living sacrifices to God" and as we are transformed by renewing our minds, our attitudes will change. List at least five godly attitudes mentioned in this passage.

sincere love, honor one another, joyful in hope, patient, faithful generous, humble, peaceful forgiving

5. Read Hebrews 4:12-16. According to this passage, what help is available to us as we seek to change ungodly attitudes?

The Word of God!

IV: APPLICATION FOR GROWTH

1. Reread the statement you wrote in section II. Now read the list of characteristics of Christ's attitudes from Philippians 2 (section III-2). How can you apply these Christlike attitudes to your own situation? What kind of thoughts will you need to think in order to begin to change your wrong attitudes?

2. Scan the attitudes listed in Romans 12:1-3 and 9-21. Are you convicted about a certain attitude in your life that needs to be transformed? What would be the benefits of changing this attitude?

tolerance and forgiveness less stress

3. Review Hebrews 4:12-16 (see section III-5). How can these truths help you transform ugly attitudes into lovely attitudes?

V: CHALLENGE FOR CHANGE

Select at least one challenge to put into practice this week.

1. Pray regularly and specifically about your wrong attitudes, asking for God's help (Hebrews 4:16) and work in you (Philippians 2:13).

2. Select one verse from God's Word that will help you transform a wrong attitude by renewing your mind (Romans 12:2). Read it often. Memorize it. Think about it.

3. Read Philippians 2:5-11 every day this week. Meditate on Christ's attitudes as described in this passage. How can His example help you have the right attitudes as you face problem situations?

4. Evaluate what kind of thoughts (seeds) have contributed to these ugly attitudes (weeds!). Reject the wrong thoughts that Satan wants to plant! Plant the seeds listed in Philippians 4:8.

FINISHING TOUCHES

THE TINT OF our attitudes can color us ugly or lovely. Attitudes that reflect Christ in and through us will be submissive, humble, serving. Stubbornness, pride, and self-centeredness will taint the canvas on which God is trying to paint the colors of true righteousness and holiness, as Ephesians 4:24 states. Let's continually ask God to reveal to us our unholy attitudes so that we can confess them. We need to fix our thoughts on those things that will help us, as portraits of loveliness, reflect the One Who is the loveliest of all.

The Color of Our Words

IN ANY PORTRAIT, one quality or feature usually leaves a striking impression upon us. The Mona Lisa's mysterious smile is one example of such a feature. In the portrait of our lives, our words leave a striking impression. Perhaps you can remember being in the company of a woman who seemed beautiful: fashionably dressed, perfectly coiffured, confidently poised. But then she spoke some words—words that were perhaps hurtful, critical, complaining, indecent, or boastful—and her beauty seemed to fade because of the effect of her words.

The color of our words is of great concern to the Lord. How do we know? Because the Bible says so much about this topic! The book of James asserts frankly, "If any man among you seem to be religious, and bridleth not his tongue, but deceiveth his own heart, this man's religion is vain" (James 1:26). James 3:2 states, "For in many things we offend all. If any man offend not in word, the same is a perfect man, and able also to bridle the whole body." As we can see from these verses, the challenge of using godly speech is an on-going one.

This lesson touches just the tip of the iceberg with regard to what the Bible says about words. If this study helps you begin to address any problems in this area of your life, use a concordance to continue studying and learning what God says about your words. Remember, what you SAY will STAY with those who hear your voice!

I: VERSE FOR MEMORIZATION AND MEDITATION

"Let no corrupt communication proceed out of your mouth, but that which is good to the use of edifying, that it may minister grace unto the hearers" (Ephesians 4:29).

1. What kind of words are corrupt or unwholesome?

curse words, profanity, boasting

2. What words in the verse describe what our speech ought to be?

wholesome, building up

II: EVALUATION FOR PREPARATION

Proverbs 25:11 states, "A word fitly spoken is like apples of gold in pictures of silver." Gold and silver are shining, captivating, and valuable. Think about your words in general—at home with your family, at work, on the phone with friends, and other situations. How would you complete the following sentence?

I think the Lord would want my words to ___*glorify Him,*___

___*encourage others*_____

_____

Words come from thoughts and attitudes of the heart. How are your thoughts and attitudes affecting your words?

III: SCRIPTURES FOR STUDY

1. Read the following passages and describe how each woman used her words to do evil.

Eve—Genesis 3:2-6

lied, sounded harsh (made God) to accomplish her own desires

Rebekah—Genesis 27:6-29

lied to gain her own ends

Potiphar's wife—Genesis 39:7-20

lied against Joseph who wound up in jail

Delilah—Judges 16:4-19

money

Sapphira—Acts 5:1-10

lying for personal gain

2. Read the following passages and describe how each woman used her words to do good.

Deborah—Judges 4:4-10; 5:1, 2

Praised God

Ruth—Ruth 1:14-18

showed love & loyalty

Esther—Esther 4:7-9, 16; 5:1-5; 7:1-6

used her influence to help God's people

Samaritan woman—John 4:28-30, 39

used her words as testimony for Jesus

Priscilla—Acts 18:24-26

explained God's word to others

3. Read James 3:2. What is an evidence that we can control our bodies?

We can all control ourselves with God's help & guidance

4. Scan James 3:1—4:17 and list the ways in which words can be destructive. Note any references to attitudes that might cause such words to be spoken.

hurtful - in retaliation "getting even"

5. Why do you think James wrote so much about words?

This is the way we reach others - we can encourage, lift up, praise, enlighten, build up or discourage, tear down, hurt, wound or destroy others by the words we speak!

6. Why did God include this topic in His Word?

Because this is a very important part of our daily lives & we can control it if we will.

7. Read Ephesians 4:20—5:21. According to this passage, in what ways can words be evil?

Anything said in anger, rage bitterness or slander is not according to the law we are expected to show others!

8. According to Ephesians 4:20—5:1, how can words be edifying?

Speak only those words that will encourage & build up others.

9. Relate Ephesians 4:22-24 to the topic of words, giving specific examples, if possible.

IV: APPLICATION FOR GROWTH

1. Scan the James passage again (3:1—4:17). Does one particular problem with words seem applicable to your life right now? What negative attitudes have a direct relation to this problem? What counsel given in the passage could help you in overcoming this problem?

frustration at attitudes
unforgiveness of hurtful words & situations
We all stumble & must seek God's help
& guidance to overcome our stupidity

2. Scan the Ephesians passage again (4:20—5:21). The instructions of this passage were given by Paul to church members to teach them how to behave toward one another. How will the counsel about words strengthen and help a church? How could it also apply to our home situations? conver-sations with friends?

If we view others
with love & kindness, it is much easier
to forgive & overlook the little things that
seem so upsetting & disturbing allowing
the loving attitude to grow

3. Reread the statement you wrote in section II. List any commands from the Ephesians passage that will help you make necessary changes.

Put off your old self! Don't be quick to
judge others & find fault - become angry.
Be More like Christ in thought & actions!

V: CHALLENGE FOR CHANGE

Select at least one challenge to put into practice this week.

1. Write Ephesians 4:29 on a card and post it in a place where you will see it often. Memorize this verse. Think about situations when you will need to put this verse into practice. *Do not let any unwholesome talk come out of your mouths but only what is helpful for building others up according to their needs that it may benefit those who listen.*

2. Commit your problem with words to God in prayer, asking Him to help you live in the victory over this sin that Christ already secured for you on the cross. (Realize that you need to prepare yourself for this battle every day!) Don't forget to ask His forgiveness and the forgiveness of anyone you may have hurt by your words. Ask the Lord to bring to your mind verses that will help you. Pray especially about attitudes that may be causing your problem with words.

3. List two teachings from Ephesians and James that you found most helpful in dealing with your problem with words. Read these at least twice daily this week. Try to put these Scriptural commands into practice and evaluate your words often.

FINISHING TOUCHES

AS WE HAVE SEEN, the Lord wants our words to shine forth as silver and gold: peaceable, considerate, merciful, truthful, helpful, kind, pure, and full of song, thanksgiving, and praise. In our portraits our words can "color us ugly" or "color us lovely." As our words are aptly spoken, the Master Painter will be able to wash over our portraits untarnishing glimmers of gold and silver. What a wonderful impression this will leave on those who view the portraits of our lives!

L E S S O N   7

The Color of Actions

W E HAVE ALREADY SEEN that the outlines of our portraits will be shaped by our thoughts. Our thoughts, in turn, will determine our attitudes, which will express themselves in our words and actions. These are the colors of the portraits of our lives.

As in all areas of life, the Lord Jesus Christ is the model for our actions. We gain deeper insight if we study and glean from Scripture the thought patterns of our Savior. In John 4:34 He declared, "My meat is to do the will of him that sent me." His prayer in John 12:28 was "Father, glorify thy name." From these thoughts proceeded His God-glorifying and pleasing actions. Because He wanted to do His Father's will, He always did what was right. His perfect actions revealed His perfect holiness and His perfect love for God and others.

You are not perfect, but your actions will reveal whether your heart is focused upon yourself and your desires or upon glorifying God and expressing His love to others. Spirit-led actions, which are a blend of doing God's will and showing God's love, are true and beautiful colors indeed!

I: VERSE FOR MEMORIZATION AND MEDITATION

"In this the children of God are manifest, and the children of the devil: whosoever doeth not righteousness is not of God, neither he that loveth not his brother" (1 John 3:10).

1. Read this verse in its context, 1 John 3:7-10. What does it mean to "do righteousness"? *To do the right thing in God's eyes*

47

2. How do we know what is right? *By listening & studying God's word*

3. Is this verse saying that Christians will never sin? Explain your answer. *No - but if you are God's child you will try very hard to please Him & do His will.*

4. What two kinds of actions reveal a person's faith in God?
The way they live and their love for others. attitudes - deeds

II: EVALUATION FOR PREPARATION

Is there a specific person or group of people toward whom you have a hard time acting righteously and lovingly? What thoughts and attitudes are causing this problem? *Yes - a bit of sinful nature that is still in my life.*

III: SCRIPTURES FOR STUDY

1. Each of the following verses describes some aspect of our Savior's actions. Jot down what it is.

John 8:29 *Always pleasing the Father*

John 13:2-5 *A servants heart*

John 14:31 *Loving the Father & doing exactly what He commands*

Acts 10:38   *doing good & healing those under Satan's power*

John 17:4   *Completing the work God gave him to do*

John 19:25-27   *Love and honor shown his Mother*

1 Peter 2:23   *didn't try to "get even"*

2. Read Galatians 5:19-21. This list is the *works* (actions) of the flesh. Jot down the words. Look up the definition for any word you do not know.   *Sexual immorality, impurity, debauchery idolatry, witchcraft hatred, discord, jealousy fits of rage, selfish ambitions, dissentions factions   envy, drunkenness, orgies*

3. Read Galatians 5:22 and 23. These qualities are called "fruit." Why is this a better word than "works"?

Because these qualities are results of our "works"!

4. How does Galatians 5:19-23 agree with the memory verse, 1 John 3:10?   *If we love God and do righteous deeds to please Him our lives will show these qualities*

5. Read Romans 13:8-14. What are the things we will NOT do if we are acting with love toward God and others? *adultry, murder, steal, covet, anything that would bring harm to another!*

6. Read Romans 13:8-14 again. What commands are given for us to obey that will result in ACTIONS of love? *love thy neighbor as thyself!*

7. What are two motivating factors for right actions mentioned in Romans 13:8-14? *Love Your Neighbor Clothe yourself in the Lord Jesus*

IV: APPLICATION FOR GROWTH

1. What ungodly actions listed in Galatians 5:19-21 may be done subtly and be hard to detect? Give a specific illustration, if possible.

2. The qualities listed in Galatians 5:22 and 23 are demonstrated not only by actions, but also by attitudes because they guide us to respond in a certain way to the circumstances of life (e.g., an attitude of love, an attitude of self-control). Give examples of how four of these attitudes will display themselves in our actions. *Peace - Kindness - Self control Faithfullness*

3. How will doing the things listed in verses 19-21 affect
YOU? SNEAKY - DECIETFUL

OTHERS? HURT

YOUR TESTIMONY FOR CHRIST?
DESTROY

4. How will actions that reflect the fruit in Galatians 5:22 and 23
affect
YOU? SERENITY - PEACE

OTHERS? TRUST - LOVE

YOUR TESTIMONY FOR CHRIST?
STRENGTHEN

5. Choose one quality of the fruit listed in Galatians 5:22 and 23 and give a specific instance when Jesus demonstrated this fruit by His actions. In what specific way can you do the same? (Consider especially the person or people you listed in section II.)

V: CHALLENGE FOR CHANGE

Select at least one challenge to put into practice this week.

1. Write a motto from your list in section III-6 that will help you act as you should. Post it in at least one prominent place as a reminder to act out of love for God and others.

2. Become more at ease with saying, "I'm sorry. Will you forgive me for acting _____." (Having to say this a few times may help restrain you from acting hurtfully again.) Do you need to say this to someone today? Be sure to ask God's forgiveness as well.

3. Do you have an "enemy" or someone with whom you have trouble getting along? How can you "do good" to this person this week? Here are some suggestions: (1) pray daily for that person (Luke 6:27, 28); (2) keep a check on your thoughts and attitudes about that person; (3) ask the Spirit to help you act in love toward this one.

FINISHING TOUCHES

WHEN IT COMES to our actions, it could very well be said, "Be careful! Your heart is showing!" Our actions often reveal our weak spots in our relationship with God. They are an indication of the extent to which we are "filled with Spirit" (Ephesians 5:18) and evidencing the Spirit's fruit. They show how much (or how little) we love others. Our actions reveal, sooner or later, who we *really* are. We may pretend to be holy, as the Pharisees of Jesus' day did (Matthew 15:7, 8), but eventually all the unholiness of the heart will work its way out. We may put a patch of pretty color over the ugly spots in our portraits, but it will wear off, and the truth about us will be revealed! Only the Master Painter can remove the spots of deep-rooted sin and self-centeredness and apply the attractive colors of sincere love in action. We will show forth His colors as we do right and love in deed and in truth.

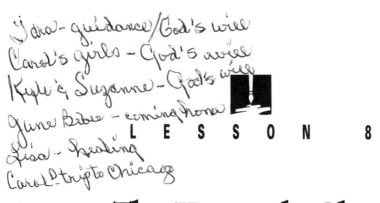

Tara - guidance/God's will
Carol's girls - God's will
Kyle & Suzanne - God's will
June Babee - coming home
Lisa - healing
Carol - trip to Chicago

L E S S O N 8

The Heavenly Glow of Our Good Deeds

OUTSIDE BIBLICAL CHRISTIANITY is a world trying to earn its way into Heaven by doing good deeds. Although these works are done from many different motivations (fear, guilt, pride, or—at best—human altruism), they are not done for the glory of God. They do not have their roots in a Spirit-indwelt and controlled person.

The Lord expects good deeds from His children—*after* salvation by faith in His Son! These good deeds are not a means to get us into Heaven (Titus 3:5), but a reflection of Heaven in us, a "light" to shine before the world to direct its attention to God (Matthew 5:16).

What will differentiate the works of the world from the works of the child of God? Even as believers, we realize the difficulty of doing kind acts from the proper motivation. Of what do Biblical good deeds consist? What purpose do they serve in God's plan for us? What are the sources of true good deeds? What should be our motives and attitudes while doing them? A daughter of God needs to answer these questions if she desires her works of kindness to shed traces of heavenly light over the portrait of her life. And, as always, she needs to go to God's own Word to find the answers to these questions.

I: VERSE FOR MEMORIZATION AND MEDITATION

"Let your light so shine before men, that they may see your good works, and glorify your Father which is in heaven" (Matthew 5:16).

1. Read Matthew 5:1, 2, and 14-16. What is the context, or setting, of Matthew 5:16? Who spoke these words?

Sermon on the mount.

Jesus

2. To whom were these words spoken?

disciples

3. What do you think it means to "let your light shine"?

let people see the love of Christ shine in you.

II: EVALUATION FOR PREPARATION

Consider a good deed you did this past week. What was your motive for doing it? What was your attitude while doing it? Do you think this good work was pleasing to God? Did it bring glory to Him?

To give help - joy - yes - yes

III: SCRIPTURES FOR STUDY

1. The following verses are a partial list of some of the good works God desires us to do. What sort of deeds should we be doing?

Proverbs 31:20

helping the needy

Luke 10:33, 34

physical help, compassion

Acts 9:36, 39

helping the poor - giving them clothes

Romans 12:13

share with the needy
show hospitality

2 Corinthians 1:10, 11

pray for others

Galatians 6:2

carry each others burdens

1 Timothy 5:9, 10

helping older widows

1 Timothy 6:17-19

teaching others about God & to put their hope & trust in Him

James 1:27

look after orphans & widows & keep ourselves from being influenced by the world

2. What are the means, or resources, that enable us to do true good works?

John 15:4, 5

staying close to God thru Jesus dwell in Him

Romans 12:6-8

close fellowship with other believers - helping & encouraging one another thru the special gifts God has given

2 Corinthians 9:8 God will supply us with what we need to do His work thru His grace

Galatians 5:22, 23

The Holy Spirit

Ephesians 2:8-10

God's grace

Ephesians 4:11, 12

God's gifts

2 Thessalonians 1:11

prayers of others
God's power

2 Timothy 2:20, 21

U...

2 Timothy 3:16, 17

the scriptures

James 3:17

God given wisdom

3. What are some of the purposes God accomplishes through our good deeds and service to others?

Matthew 5:16

that others might see God's love thru us & therefore praise Him

Ephesians 4:11-13

helps to prepare us and others to build up and bring together all in the faith to grow in knowledge of Him

1 Timothy 2:9, 10

To clothe ourselves with the imperisable quality of a gentle & quiet spirit which is precious in the sight of God!

James 2:17, 18

to demonstrate our faith to others What we do for others is who we are & to whom we belong

1 Peter 2:12

live your lives in such a way that they cannot deny the glory of God.

1 Peter 4:10

whatever gift God has given - use it to bring God glory

4. Carefully read the following verses, looking for motives and attitudes that should characterize our acts of service for others. Jot down what you find in each passage.

Luke 10:25-37 *Loving the LORD with your whole being will cause you to obey His commands of loving and caring for others*

Acts 2:42-47

Fellowshiping with sisters and brothers in Christ to encourage and build up one another to praise & worship God & enjoying each others company

Acts 4:32-37

willingness to give and share with others so that none are needy needlessly

Philippians 2:3-7

likemindness with Christ be not selfish or vain - but humble in attitude - a servants heart

James 3:13

humility from wisdom

1 John 3:16-18; 5:2

love

IV: APPLICATION FOR GROWTH

1. What do you think is the primary spiritual requirement that is the basis for any good deeds that we do? (Review John 15:4 and 5.)

Love of God & desire to do His commands

2. List three key motives for service to others based on the Scriptures you studied. *Please the LORD*

Love for others

self sacrifice

3. What wrong motives may lie behind some believers' good works?

personal recognaction

personal gain

4. The two Acts passages in section III-4 portray amazingly high standards of Christian conduct. What one quality (relating to good works) particularly strikes and challenges you? Why?

5. With so many needs surrounding us, how can we know what good deeds God wants us to do? *those We equipd us to do*

6. Choose one area of service from the list in section III-1 in which you are challenged to do more. *teaching others*

V: CHALLENGE FOR CHANGE

Select at least one challenge to put into practice this week.

Check the ways in which your "deeds doing" needs to change.

1. I need to do more works of service for others.

2. I need to do fewer deeds in order to fulfill my other priorities.

3. I need to do good deeds from proper, Biblical motives.

4. I need to be more cautious about my attitudes with regard to my good deeds.

5. I need to strengthen my spiritual life as the source of my good deeds.

6. I need to seek God's will in prayer daily as to what I ought to do for others.

7. I need to determine my spiritual gift to use as God leads me, administering His grace to others.

8. I need to improve some relationships with believers in order to serve with unity, love, and holiness.

Commit this change to God in prayer.

FINISHING TOUCHES

WHEN IT COMES to doing good, love is the key: love for God and love for others. Our works should proceed from a heart of love for Christ and a desire to obey Him. As we love others, in obedience to His command, we will do works of service for them. Our faith and our love will be displayed through our actions, not just our words.

For whom are we to do good works? Galatians 6:10 says, "As we have therefore opportunity, let us do good unto all men, especially unto them who are of the household of faith." We could be very busy!

Let us not, however, be so busy that we "leave our first love." (Please read Revelation 2:1, 2, and 4.) We must not neglect our personal relationship with the Lord or our other responsibilities, such as caring for a husband and children. We need wisdom from God to determine the balance of our priorities.

Our good deeds are our "heavenly light." Let us allow the Master Painter to "highlight" our portraits with glimmers of heavenly light that come from true good works, "which becometh women professing godliness" (1 Timothy 2:10).

Attention to Details:
Our Appearance

T HE FOCAL POINTS of our portraits are our thoughts, attitudes, words, and actions. However, to complete the total picture, the peripheral details of our lives also need to mesh with God's total design for us. We need to pay attention to these details so that they will enhance, not detract from, the beauty of the Master's work in us. One such detail is our outward appearance.

To approach the topic of our outward appearance is to tread on sensitive ground. Some aspects of our physical appearance have been determined by God and are generally unchangeable. But some aspects of our outward appearance are a matter of choice and taste, and some deal with convictions that will vary in as many ways as there are Christian women. However, just because a certain topic may be a sensitive one, should we avoid discussing it? If the Bible is not silent on the issue (and it's not), then we need to consider what God says about our outward appearance and, in obedience to Him, make any needed changes as He convicts us to do so. To be women of God means every aspect of our lives comes under His scrutiny. Let us examine ourselves as we study the general principles of His Word.

I: VERSES FOR MEMORIZATION AND MEDITATION

"Whose adorning let it not be that outward adorning of plaiting the hair, and of wearing of gold, or of putting on of apparel; But let it be the hidden man of the heart, in that which is not corruptible, even the ornament of a meek and

quiet spirit, which is in the sight of God of great price" (1 Peter 3:3, 4).

1. Do these verses teach that we should disregard our physical appearance? Explain what you think the verses mean. *No*

We should be neat, clean, modest, appropriately dressed but that true beauty comes from within

2. According to these verses, what qualities is God seeking to paint into the portrait of our lives?

peace, joy, quiet spirit, love of our Heavenly Father!

II: EVALUATION FOR PREPARATION

Suppose for a moment that you have just been introduced to a woman about your age. Would some aspects of her appearance deter you from wanting to get to know her? What outward factors might encourage your efforts toward friendship?

III: SCRIPTURES FOR STUDY

1. Each of the following verses says something about what is reflected in a person's face. Jot down your observations next to each reference.

Genesis 4:4, 5 *Cain was very angry - his face was downcast (unhappy)*

Nehemiah 2:1, 2 *Nehemiah's heart was sad & it showed in his face*

Proverbs 7:10, 13

the prostitute was loud & defiant – her brazenness showed in her face

Ecclesiastes 8:1

wisdom brightens a man's face

Isaiah 3:8, 9

their faces showed defiance to the LORD proclaims their bold sin

Daniel 7:28

Daniel's face turned pale because he was troubled

2. What words might be an apt description of a godly woman's face?
Proverbs 15:13

Cheerful

Proverbs 15:30

cheerful

Psalm 34:4, 5 *radiant*

2 Corinthians 3:18 *the glory of the LORD should show on our face*

3. Based on all these verses, write a brief statement about the importance of our facial expressions in terms of our outward appearance.

don't go around looking like a "gloomy gus"

4. What general principle about our appearance as women can you derive from these verses: Genesis 1:27; Deuteronomy 22:5; 1 Corinthians 11:14-16? *God like*
Not act like something we're not

5. Four qualities should be reflected in our outward appearance. Find them in 1 Timothy 2:9 and 10 and Proverbs 11:22. Look up the words in a dictionary and jot down your findings.
modesty - not extreme
decency - proper conduct, speech, behavior
propriety - being proper or fitting
discretion - being careful about what
one does or says

6. Each of the following passages teaches us something about our outward appearance. Answer the questions after each reference.

Matthew 6:28-33. Why should we not be preoccupied about our clothing? Is God against beauty? *Because it is not*
the outward appearance we
should worry about but how
we show what's in our hearts
No He is not!

Isaiah 3:16-24. What are some of the reasons that the Lord was angry with the women of Zion? *they were haughty -*
flirty - indiscrete, wiseful + wanton

1 Corinthians 6:19, 20. How will the teaching contained in these verses affect the way you groom yourself?

IV: APPLICATION FOR GROWTH

1. Much of what is going on inside us will show on our faces. What are some practical things a woman of God can do to look cheerful and radiant? *Be clean, well kept, have a close relationship with Him. Don't be prideful*

2. God created two distinct sexes, and He desires a clear line of demarcation between the two. Recent trends in our society have tended to erase that line in many ways and have applied pressure toward a unisex culture. In what ways can we properly affirm the concept of femininity by our appearance within our culture today?

3. Pick one of the four qualities listed in section III-5. How does this characteristic affect
a woman's clothing?

Body properly covered

the way a woman's hair looks?

no wild fads! clean & well kept

her general appearance?

Not call attention to yourself, not overly provocative

4. Write a summary of how our physical appearance should befit the "temple of the Holy Spirit." List any additional ingredients that make an appearance that is honoring to God.

Dress in such a way as to not be ashamed to meet the Lord face to face

V: CHALLENGE FOR CHANGE

Select at least one challenge to put into practice this week.

1. Pray about this matter. Are you anxious about clothes or outward beauty? (Note that the model woman in Proverbs 31 was not described as beautiful.) Ask the Lord to bring to your attention any wrong attitudes/ aspects concerning outward appearance that He would have you adjust to reflect more perfectly His holiness in you.

2. Consider asking the opinion of someone close to you if he or she could suggest any changes in dress/hairstyle/general appearance that would better reflect femininity, modesty, and propriety. Keep these qualities in mind as you select clothes, hairstyles, or any aspect of outward adorning.

3. Take a personal inventory of the areas discussed in this lesson. Has the Holy Spirit convicted you about some aspect of your outward appearance? If so, specify what it is.

How can you begin to make needed changes? Do you know someone who can help you? What steps can you take to carry out your commitment to make these changes?

FINISHING TOUCHES

When you first read the title of this Bible study, *God's Portrait of a Beautiful Woman,* did you think first of outward beauty or inner beauty? In 1 Samuel 16:7 the Lord says, "For the Lord seeth not as man seeth; for man looketh on the outward appearance, but the Lord looketh on the heart." As women of God, we want first of all to please the Lord by the condition of our hearts. But as this verse implies, people are also looking at our outward appearance and evaluating us by what they see. Actually, what they see will tell them about who we are and what we value in life.

Two extremes must be avoided, it seems, when it comes to our outward appearance. One is a display of ostentation and worldliness by lavish, faddish dress. The other extreme is looking like an unmade bed and reflecting an I-don't-care-what-I-look-like attitude. Neither of these is befitting a woman of God who supposedly has her heart set "on things above" (Colossians 3:2) yet serves a God Who is not a God of confusion, but of peace (1 Corinthians 14:33).

We have also seen that our faces should be the focal point of our appearance and that what we are on the inside will be reflected there. Our faces should reflect radiance and joy. Whatever diverts the focus of attention from our faces is an aspect of adorning that is out of balance.

Is God against beauty? Just look at His creation! It teems with beauty. The Lord is not against beauty, but we must remember that inward beauty takes precedence over outward beauty. God IS against pride, worldliness, self-centeredness, immodesty, impropriety, indecency, and indiscretion!

God has created us to be women. Our outward appearance ought to reflect that special purpose of His design by our femininity but within the bounds of the specifications set forth in His Word. Don't overlook these small but important details of the portrait of your life.

Nov. 8th
Tara & children
Darryl

L E S S O N   1 0

Attention to Details: Our Use of Time

T HE MASTER has given each of us one resource that we often take for granted: TIME. Our use (stewardship) of this resource is another detail of our portraits that we must not overlook. Most of us would readily admit to being busy, but what are we accomplishing with our lives? We often hear words like "priorities" and "quality time," and these words imply the need for discernment.

What on earth should we be doing with our time? God cares about this, and therefore we should also. Perhaps this lesson will help us reevaluate our use of time and lead us to make some adjustments that will make our portraits, in every way, more pleasing to the Master.

I: VERSES FOR MEMORIZATION AND MEDITATION

"See then that ye walk circumspectly, not as fools, but as wise, redeeming the time, because the days are evil. Wherefore be ye not unwise, but understanding what the will of the Lord is" (Ephesians 5:15–17).

1. What two types of people are contrasted in these verses?

wise - unwise

2. What phrases describe the way God wants us to live with regard to our time?

make use of every opportunity

II: EVALUATION FOR PREPARATION

Take a few minutes to jot down what you consider to be six to eight daily priorities or responsibilities in your life. Number these in order of importance.

1 Prayer   4 helping/serving others
2 Bible study   7 cooking
6 keeping house   5 being a friend
3 personal hygiene

III: SCRIPTURES FOR STUDY

1. To what is the span of life compared in each of these verses?
1 Chronicles 29:15

like a shadow without hope

Psalm 39:5

a mere handbreadth -

Psalm 102:11

the evening shadow

James 4:14

a mist

2. Read the following passages. State how the person/people spoken of had a wrong attitude about the use of time.
Luke 12:16-21

living for tomorrow

Luke 12:42-47

use your time as tho' the Lord is coming at any moment

James 4:13-16 *Don't make plans without including the Lord*

3. With regard to the use of time, what warnings or advice are given in Scripture?

2 Thessalonians 3:11, 12

Don't be idle as this gives way to "busybodies" nosey, gossiping

1 Timothy 5:13, 14

manage our homes and give no space to idleness

Proverbs 6:6-11

Stay busy with the things that need to be taken care of - don't be lazy

Proverbs 12:24, 27

take care of your friendships, encourage others, don't be led astray by the world

4. What beneficial uses of time are presented in the following verses? What do some of these verses tell us about the Lord Jesus' priorities?

Mark 6:30, 31

spend time alone with Jesus w/God

Mark 6:45, 46

spend time in prayer

Luke 18:15-17

make time for the children in your life.

John 4:4-30

show love to others by telling them about Jesus

Acts 17:11

study the scriptures daily

Psalm 119:97

meditate on the law of the lord

1 Thessalonians 4:11

lead a quiet life, mind your own business, keep your hands busy

1 Timothy 5:9, 10, 14

being faithful, showing hospitality serving others — give no one reason to find fault with our lives

Titus 2:3-5

live our lives reverently making good examples to younger women be pleasant & kind

Hebrews 10:25

gather together with other Christian women to encourage & lift up each other.

5. Each of the following women of the Bible is commended. How did each one use her time wisely?

Ruth—Ruth 2:2-7

by working in the fields to provide for herself and Naomi

The virtuous woman—Proverbs 31:10-31

sees to the needs of her family & friends hard working - good steward uses common sense & takes care of the needy

Dorcas—Acts 9:36-39

always doing good & seeing to the needs of others. She was well remembered

Women Paul knew—Romans 16:3, 6, 12

workers in the church - hard workers for the LORD

6. How can we know how to use our time wisely and to prioritize our varying responsibilities?

Psalm 90:12

ask the LORD to teach us

James 1:5

ask God!

Psalm 119:169, 170

Pray to the LORD

Proverbs 19:20

listen to advice and accept instruction

IV: APPLICATION FOR GROWTH

1. Looking back over the Scripture passages in this lesson, write a

brief summary statement about the ways in which God would NOT have us use our time. *Don't be idle, don't carry tales about others (gossip) don't be lazy- uncaring*

2. From whom can you get advice regarding how you might more effectively use your time (Proverbs 19:20)? *others - The LORD mature christians*

3. We need wisdom to discern between what is good and what is best (Psalm 90:12). Look again at your list of priorities in section II. Reevaluate your numbering in terms of importance. What are some of the good things that may have been causing you to neglect the BEST things?

V: CHALLENGE FOR CHANGE

Select at least one challenge to put into practice this week.

1. Take a time-use inventory and make a plan for change where necessary. (Tackle one change at a time!)

2. Do you neglect a time of daily prayer and Scripture reading? If so, how can you change this? (Specify a detailed plan.)

3. Do you understand, relatively clearly, your God-given priorities, based on seeking God's will in prayer, Scripture, and counsel from others? If not, begin to do this as a basis for your proper use of time.

4. Are the activities that consume most of your daily time helping you to fulfill your responsibilities as a woman of God, a helpmeet to your

husband, a mother to your children, a member of your church, etc.? If not, how can you change this?

5. Does the bulk of your daily time revolve around material things: buying, getting, fussing with, reveling in, planning for? (Check the amount of time you spend thinking about these things.) If so, how can you change this?

6. Are any of your daily activities out of line with God's will? If so, how can you change this? What God-honoring activities can you put in their place?

7. Do you create "idle time" that you spend being a gossip/busybody, neglecting more fruitful activities? If so, how can you change this?

FINISHING TOUCHES

YOU HAVE PROBABLY HEARD the motto, "Only one life, 'twill soon be past. Only what's done for Christ will last." This thought is similar to the one expressed in 1 John 2:17: "And the world passeth away, and the lust thereof: but he that doeth the will of God abideth for ever."

It is folly to build our lives around the trifles of this world that will pass away—what a waste! I once heard it said that only two things on earth will last forever: people and the Word of God. That thought has stayed with me as I consider my use of time. God has given each person work to do, but even that can be committed to bring about the eternal purposes of God. For example, as a full-time homemaker, much of my time is taken up with tasks that revolve around material things (clothes, dishes, beds, etc.), but these things should be used to meet the basic needs of people (my family) and not as an end in themselves (materialism). Each of us should be using our time to store up treasure in Heaven (Matthew 6:20, 21), for how we use our time shows what is important to us.

We need wisdom and discernment from the Master; for example, we need sleep and rest, but not excessive sleep and idleness. God has given us time, and in the portrait of our lives, He can best direct our use of it in order to accomplish His purposes.

As I approach mid-life, I desire to be fruitful for the Lord in my use of time. Two passages in Psalms have spoken strikingly to me about this: "LORD, make me to know mine end, and the measure of my days, what it is; that I may know how frail I am. Behold, thou hast made my days as an hand breadth; and mine age is as nothing before thee: verily every man at his best state is altogether vanity. Selah. Surely every man walketh in a vain shew: surely they are disquieted in vain: he heapeth up riches, and knoweth not who shall gather them. And now, Lord, what wait I for? my hope is in thee" (Psalm 39:4-7). "Incline my heart unto thy testimonies, and not to covetousness. Turn away mine eyes from beholding vanity" (Psalm 119:36, 37).

As daughters of God, we should want our lives to be different from the daughters of the world. This difference should be reflected in our use of time—not wasting it on worthless things, but using it to accomplish God's will. Worthless things will in no way enhance the portrait of my life or yours. So let's use our time on those things that will truly make each one of us God's portrait of a beautiful woman.

L E S S O N   1 1

The Color of Relationships

THE SEVENTEENTH-CENTURY English poet and preacher John Donne wrote that famous phrase, "No man is an island." Since the day of your birth, you have been thrust into various relationships with all different kinds of people.

Because God desires us to live in fellowship with other people, despite our differences, the color of our relationships takes continual blending by the Master's hand. Some relationships blend smoothly and easily, while the colors of others tend to clash and need much work from the One Who is painting the portraits of our lives. And because the quality of our human relationships is of primary concern to Him, His Word is overflowing with principles to help us deal with all the variations of personalities, factors, and problems we may encounter.

People are eternal. They are worth the time and effort we must put into developing good relationships. Dealing with some people will stretch you to a point of total dependence on God. Relationships with other people will bring a natural overflow of blessing and gratitude. As you put into practice the relationship principles of His Word, the Master Painter will use both of these kinds of people, and more, to perfect the portrait of your life.

I: VERSE FOR MEMORIZATION AND MEDITATION

"As we have therefore opportunity, let us do good unto all men, especially unto them who are of the household of faith" (Galatians 6:10).

1. What two groups of people are mentioned by the apostle Paul?

saved & unsaved

Hebrews 10: 23-24

2. What are we to do for them? *Do good for all*

II: EVALUATION FOR PREPARATION

What particular relationship would you like to improve in your life?
What kinds of attitudes would help improve it? what kinds of words?
what kinds of actions?

III: SCRIPTURES FOR STUDY

1. We have relationships with two different groups of people—saved
and unsaved. What guidelines are given in the following passages to help
us in our relationships with people who do not belong to Christ?

1 Corinthians 9:19-23

become a servant

Colossians 4:5, 6

wise and full of grace

Titus 3:1, 2

subject to authority – slander no one peaceful and considerate – humble

Hebrews 12:14

live in peace w/ all & be holy

2. In Luke 6:27-36 the Lord Jesus taught us how to treat people who
treat us with enmity. Many different "action commands" are given in the
passage. They direct us how to handle such difficult relationships. List
these commands.

verse 27   love your enemies

verse 28   Bless those who curse you

verse 30   give to those who ask.

verse 31   treat others as you want to be treated

verse 35   love your enemies

verse 36   Be merciful

3. The New Testament epistles (letters) teach us concerning our relationship with the family of believers. Look up the following verses and write the KEY word or words that will help us have God-pleasing relationships. (Look up any words you don't know.)

Romans 15:5-7   unity - acceptance - be of one heart bringing glory to God.

Ephesians 5:21   submission

Ephesians 6:18   pray in the Spirit

Colossians 3:12-14   compassion, kindness, humility, gentleness, patience - forgiveness - LOVE

Colossians 3:16   let the word of God dwell in you teach & admonish

1 Thessalonians 5:14, 15   give guidance, encouragement be patient & kind

James 1:19   quick to listen, slow to speak, slow to anger

1 Peter 4:8-10   love each other, offer hospitality serve others with our God given gifts

IV: APPLICATION FOR GROWTH

1. Why are our relationships with unbelievers of such vital importance? *to let them see Christ thru us.*

2. How will the guidelines given in the verses you studied in section III-1 help to relax the strain that sometimes develops in our relationships with the unsaved? *Help to realize a lot of the way they are and act is because they don't know Christ - let them see what He has done for us.*

3. Think of one unsaved person you know. What guidelines listed in section III-1 will be particularly helpful to you in your relationship with this person? *living in peace with all don't slander anyone*

4. Think of a person with whom you have a difficult relationship. Select two of the commands of the Lord Jesus that you listed in section III-2 that you need to put into practice in order to deal properly with this person. *love your enemies treat others as you want to be treated*

5. How did the Lord Jesus personally exemplify these commands (section III-2) in His dealings with people who treated Him hurtfully?

forgiveness, love & mercy

6. Why are our relationships with believers so important?
encouraging in sharing our love for Christ exchanging of examples of His love for us.

7. Think of one person in the family of believers who has a need, or think of someone you don't know very well. What key word listed in section III-3 could help you minister to that person?   *prayer*

V: CHALLENGE FOR CHANGE

Select at least one challenge to put into practice this week.

1. Is there an unbeliever with whom you should have a better relationship? Select one practical way (based on the guidelines and commands you studied) to improve your relationship with this person. (Some examples are ask forgiveness, express sincere gratitude or admiration, do a kindness, pray for that person.) Make a commitment and DO it!

forgiveness and prayer

2. Is there a believer with whom you should have a better relationship? Select one practical way (based on the key words in section III-3 or your answer in IV-7) to improve your relationship with this person. Make a commitment and DO it!

have more compassion in your attitude/ more prayer

FINISHING TOUCHES

THE COLOR OF our relationships is a primary color in the portraits of our lives. It should be a peaceful, soothing color that, in many instances, can be created only by the Master Painter's skill. Romans 12:18 directs us, "If it be possible, as much as lieth in you, live peaceably with all men." We cannot control how others treat us, but we can control our response to them. Whether we are witnessing, working, warning, or worshiping together, we should always reflect the love and concern of the Lord Jesus Christ, the Model for our portraits.

Romans 12: 9-21

L E S S O N 1 2

The Unifying Factor: Love

ACH OF THE GREAT painters of the past had a style all his own: Van Gogh, Rembrandt, Picasso. Unique factors about their works make the paintings recognizably theirs. The short, swirling brush strokes of Van Gogh, for example, along with his use of intense, vibrant color, resulted in paintings bursting with energy and emotion.

In the portrait of a godly woman's life, certain factors—such as faith, holiness, humility, hope, and joy—will identify her as a creation of the Master. These factors will pervade every aspect of her life and clearly identify her as a new creation in Christ (2 Corinthians 5:17).

But the key factor, the unifying factor over all the areas that have been mentioned, is LOVE. Love plays a part in all these other factors, whether it be God's love for us or our love for Him. In a Bible concordance, the list of verses under the word "love" is staggering. Why so much about love? Because God in His nature is love. Since God is characterized by love, His desire for us is to reflect His love in this world also. "Beloved, let us love one another: for love is of God; and every one that loveth is born of God, and knoweth God" (1 John 4:7).

Perhaps we need to understand what love is, since our world has little concept of real love. Approaching a standard dictionary seemed a doubtful method of finding a definition that would do justice by Biblical standards, but I did find a beginning: love is "unselfish, loyal, and benevolent concern for another." The word "unselfish" is a necessary ingredient when defining real love. "Loyal concern" is good, but "steadfast commitment to" is better. Love is not based upon a feeling, but true love is based upon a decision to act continually in the best interest of another. Real love says, "I love you because I love you!" Our lives need the unifying factor of love.

I: VERSES FOR MEMORIZATION AND MEDITATION

"Put on therefore, as the elect of God, holy and beloved, bowels of mercies, kindness, humbleness of mind, meekness, longsuffering; forbearing one another, and forgiving one another, if any man have a quarrel against any: even as Christ forgave you, so also do ye. And above all these things put on charity, which is the bond of perfectness" (Colossians 3:12–14).

1. How does love bind together in a believer's life all the other virtues mentioned in these verses? *If you have Christian love the other qualities have a tendency to fall into place*

2. What motivation is mentioned for such a life?
Love as Christ loved

II: EVALUATION FOR PREPARATION

Write down how your love toward one of the people in the following list has been lacking.

God	children	friend
husband	sister	a church member
parents	brother	pastor/teacher
relative	coworker	neighbor

patience (long suffering) and forgiveness

III: SCRIPTURES FOR STUDY

1. Read 1 John 4:7—5:4. What do the following verses tell you about God and love?

verse 7 *Love comes from God*

verse 8 *If you don't love - you don't know God - God is LOVE*

verses 9, 10 *Because of His love for us He sent His son*

verse 19 *He loved us first*

2. What are some of the results of God's love in a believer's life according to that same passage?

verses 7, 11, 21 *Because of His LOVE we can love others*

verse 16 *We can live in God because of His love*

verses 17, 18 *We can be complete in His LOVE and not live in fear*

chapter 5, verse 3 *We will obey His commands*

3. What do these verses teach about loving others?

verse 12 *His LOVE is made complete in us.*

verse 20 *If we don't love our brother whom we have seen- we cannot love God*

chapter 5, verse 2 *We know we love others by loving God and carrying out His commands*

4. Read 1 Corinthians 13. Summarize in a sentence or two what the apostle Paul said about love in verses 1–3.

Without love anything else you do counts for nothing.

5. Read carefully the descriptions of love in 1 Corinthians 13:4–7.
Which descriptions pertain to our thoughts?

not self seeking – keeping no records of others wrongs

Which descriptions pertain to our attitudes?

Which descriptions pertain to our words?

*not boasting, not rude
not cause problems by untruths (gossip)*

Which descriptions pertain to our actions?

protects, pressing on (keep trying) in difficult relationships

6. What do you think is meant by "Love never fails" (v. 8)?

unconditional   God's LOVE

7. How would you explain the meaning of verse 13?

unselfish love

IV: APPLICATION FOR GROWTH

1. First John 4:19 states, "We love him, because he first loved us." Understanding and accepting God's love for us is a key issue in our spiritual birth and growth. Has it been easy or difficult for you to believe and accept that God loves you? Why or why not?

2. What may hinder us from believing God loves us?

The relationship we had with our earthly father

3. How can we better understand and receive God's love for us?

Getting to know Him from His Word

4. We need to love God before we can really love others. How can we deepen our love for the Lord? *Developing a closer relationship with Him and the WORD*

5. First John 4:7—5:4 speaks of the necessary correlation between loving God and loving others. How will your love for God enable you to love others in your thoughts, attitudes, words, and actions?

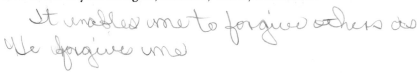

It enables me to forgive others as He forgives me

6. Does one particular verse speak strongly to you about loving others? Which one?

4/5

7. The unifying factor of love reveals itself in many ways, as listed in
1 Corinthians 13:4-7. From the qualities listed in that passage, select one
that you especially need to put into practice—perhaps toward the person
you listed in section II. *keeps no record of wrongs*

V: CHALLENGE FOR CHANGE

Select at least one challenge to put into practice this week.

1. We need to continually deepen our love for the Lord. The Lord
Jesus Himself said that this was the first and greatest commandment
(Matthew 22:37, 38). We love Him more as we think about what He is
like and what He has done for us. (See Psalm 116 and Isaiah 53, for
example.) We show our love for Him by obeying His Word to the best of
our ability as the Spirit helps us. The more we love Him, the more that
love will overflow to others. Surround yourself daily with reminders of
His love for you: verses, music, books, or a blessings list.

2. Have you prided yourself on some God-given talent or ability?
Remember, if you are not acting in love, such abilities are empty. (Love
isn't proud, and love doesn't boast!) Always keep in mind that love is the
supreme and greatest gift, the most excellent way. It is ministering to
meet the needs of others. Only in the context of love do our gifts and
talents fulfill their God-intended purpose. Evaluate your motives for
service. Ask the Lord to help you serve out of a heart of love for Him and
others.

3. Read again 1 Corinthians 13:4-7. Commit yourself to demonstrate
the unifying factor of love to the person you listed in section II. Ask God
for help. Ask that person's forgiveness, if necessary. Write out the quality
you selected in IV-7 and post it as a reminder of your commitment.

FINISHING TOUCHES

THE PORTRAIT CREATED by the Master's hand will inevitably reflect the style of love because God is love. If we are allowing our lives to be "perfected" by Him, His love will be evidenced in all our ways:

—by our salvation
—by our acceptance of His work in us and His Lordship over us
—by our love for His Holy Spirit and His Word
—in our Spirit-controlled thoughts
—in our godly attitudes
—in our wholesome words
—in our Christlike actions
—in our sincere good deeds
—in our proper appearance
—in our wise use of time
—in our peaceful relationships

Love unifies all of these into a life that reflects God's ownership, His signature on our portraits.

The Lord Jesus made a very weighty statement when He said, "By this shall all men know that ye are my disciples, if ye have love one to another" (John 13:35). We live in a world that is thirsting for love and looking for it in every dried-up stream. Unsaved people will be watching us, the followers of Christ. As they see genuine love overflowing from believers to one another, they will recognize it for what it is—real love. They will know that it comes from being His disciples. They will acknowledge that there is one exceptional factor that makes us dynamically different—the distinctive style of love. Are they seeing that kind of love in your life and mine? May we not fail our Lord by failing to truly love.

Framing It All with Prayer and Praise

MOST OF THE GREAT PORTRAITS that hang in museums are graced by lovely frames. The perfect frame around a painting enhances, completes, and attracts attention to the portrait itself.

The spiritually minded woman needs to encompass the portrait of her life with prayer and praise. These two *P* words are the finishing touches to the masterpiece. They enhance, richly and deeply, the Master's glorious work of grace upon us. They are necessary for our holiness. They attract the interest of others by creating a different atmosphere about us.

Every "Challenge for Change" section in this study has included a call for *prayer*. Prayer promotes the Master's work that will endure for all eternity. How vital it becomes! And every time He transforms us a little more into His portrait of a beautiful woman, we have reason to *praise*. Praise fulfills our purpose for living—to glorify God and attract the attention of others in order to direct it to the One Who can do wonderful things for them as well.

Can a woman be godly if she doesn't pray? Are we giving credit to the Master if we fail to praise? Too often, as I have found in my own life, these two activities are weak. A frame that is dull and inconspicuous fails to magnify the noteworthy qualities that the Master intended for display. Prayer and praise must issue forth from our hearts and lips to Him. If each of us is to be His complete portrait of a beautiful, spiritually mature woman, how necessary it is to frame our lives with prayer and praise!

I: VERSE FOR MEMORIZATION AND MEDITATION

"And Hannah prayed, and said, My heart rejoiceth in the LORD, mine horn is exalted in the LORD . . ." (1 Samuel 2:1).

1. For what two things did Hannah offer praise? (Read the rest of verse 1.) *for who God is and what He did for her*

2. To whom did she speak this praise? *God*

II: EVALUATION FOR PREPARATION

1. In what ways do you think your prayer life could be improved; e.g., more time, more personal prayer, more group prayer, having a prayer list, more worship, more thanksgiving?

personal prayer & group prayer (all of the above)

2. Do you find it easy or difficult to praise God for Who He is and what He has done? If this is difficult for you, can you think of why this is so? *Not as easy as it should be*

III: SCRIPTURES FOR STUDY

1. The Lord Jesus spent much time alone in prayer. If God Himself did this as He encountered the trials of life, how much more should we. What are some of the things the Lord taught His disciples to include in prayer? The references in parentheses indicate that we, too, need to include these items.

Matthew 6:9 (Psalm 103:1) *praise & worship*

Matthew 6:10 (Matthew 26:39)

Willing to yield to God's will

Matthew 6:11 (Philippians 4:19)

asking God for our daily needs

Matthew 6:12 (1 John 1:9)

confess our sin

Matthew 6:13 (John 17:15; Luke 22:40)

keep us from temptations

Matthew 5:43, 44 (Acts 7:59, 60)

our enemies

Matthew 9:38 (Colossians 4:3, 4)

for people to be soul winners for Christ

2. What are some things the apostle Paul instructed believers to pray for?

Ephesians 6:18   *for others / everything & all things*

Philippians 4:6   *be thankful and pray for everything*

1 Thessalonians 5:17, 18   *always give thanks for all things*

1 Timothy 2:1, 2 *all people even those you do not agree with and those with authority over you.*

3. What do the following Scripture passages give as reasons for giving praise, glory, and thanks to God?

Revelation 5:11, 12

God is worthy of it & deserves it

Romans 1:20, 21

Keeps us from becoming proud and arrogant (thinking we are self-sufficient)

1 Peter 2:9

It is a privilege and a command because He called us out of the darkness.

1 Thessalonians 5:18

God's will

Psalm 95:1-7 *He is our Creator, Almighty God, He loves & cares for us*

Psalm 71:14-18 *To make sure we continue the truth of His love, power, supreme being & mighty acts alive for the future*

4. We read in Acts 2:42-47 that prayer and praise played a part in the early church. How did this affect the believers as a group?

Keep them together, unified them gave them joy to fellowship with one another

Read 1 Samuel 1:1—2:11.

5. Describe how prayer helped Hannah become God's portrait of a beautiful woman. *She petitioned for her needs then trusted His will and waited on Him - gave Him praise when her needs were met*

6. In what ways did Hannah give praise to God for what He had done? *She told others of His answer to her prayers. She named her son with Samuel which means "heard by God"*

7. What are four things for which Hannah praised God in her prayer?

Who He is   His love

What He does   Saving us

IV: APPLICATION FOR GROWTH

1. As a group, discuss ways to make your personal prayer time more effective. Talk about different times to pray, ways to organize your prayer time, things for which to pray, how to overcome difficulties to prayer.

2. If a person has difficulty publicly expressing praise, how could she begin to develop more ease in doing so? *Psalms*

3. How will your prayer and praise help strengthen your local church?

4. What one aspect of Hannah's prayer and praise model can you apply to your own life? *consistancy*

V: CHALLENGE FOR CHANGE

Select at least one challenge to put into practice this week.

1. Based on your answers for section III-1 and 2, what areas of prayer do you need to strengthen in your own life? *regl'e, consistant prayer time*

2. Endeavor to praise God more this week: in prayer, verbally to others, or in a note to someone. If this is difficult for you, ask the Lord to help you praise Him more.

3. Perhaps your life is something like Hannah's. You may be facing a difficulty as great as the one Hannah faced. Are you praying about it? Are your requests within God's will? If so, commit it to prayer and then wait upon your mighty Lord for His answer (yes, no, wait). When the answer comes, thank Him (1 Thessalonians 5:18) and praise Him for Who He is— our wise, loving Heavenly Father.

FINISHING TOUCHES

Is THE FRAME around your portrait a little dull or dusty? Don't leave it that way; clean it and shine it up! Make it serve its purpose in the portrait of your life—to highlight all the facets of God's work in you. A splendid portrait with a magnificent frame lacks nothing. It is ready to be put in full view of all, without disgrace. The Master's signature will be clearly seen upon it, and He will not be ashamed for everyone to know that it belongs to Him.

C O N C L U S I O N

The Unveiling

A S WE HAVE SEEN, every woman is a creation of God. Each of us truly could have been God's portrait of a beautiful woman, but the portrait was marred by sin—the curse of sin upon mankind as well as our own sin nature and sinful acts. But God in His love, mercy, and grace had a plan to restore each one of us to our intended spiritual beauty through salvation and sanctification.

Once we become His children through faith in His Son, He works in us daily to bring His plan to completion. When will it be complete? At the moment we see Christ Jesus face to face, the masterpiece will finally be finished. The unveiling will take place. At that time every shape will be perfect, every color pure. The parts of the portrait that now don't seem to fit will make perfect sense. The unveiled portrait will reflect the very image of Christ Jesus Himself!

The lovely words of 1 John 3:2 and 3 state it this way: "Beloved, now are we the sons [children] of God, and it doth not yet appear what we shall be: but we know that, when he shall appear, we shall be like him; for we shall see him as he is. And every man that hath this hope in him purifieth himself, even as he is pure."

Until that day, may you as His daughter yield yourself to Him and be, as much as you are able, God's portrait of a beautiful woman.

LEADER'S GUIDE

SUGGESTIONS FOR LEADERS

It is my earnest desire and prayer that God would use His living Word to bring forth spiritual beauty in the women of your ladies' Bible study group. I urge you to adapt this study to meet your needs. Each group of women is unique. You as the leader will best sense how your group's spiritual needs can be met.

I have provided answers for each lesson's questions to clarify my intent and to stimulate thought. Your group's answers may differ from mine, and, in some cases, there are no right or wrong answers. The additional discussion questions in the answer section can be used as you see fit. Encourage discussion! The Holy Spirit is the best Teacher. Let Him guide and work in your group as He deems best.

I suggest that you approach each section as follows:

Introduction—Begin the study with prayer, seeking God's help as you study His Word. Use the suggested questions (see answer section) as a means to get the ladies thinking about the day's topic.

Section I—Encourage your ladies to memorize the verse or verses given. The lesson topic relates directly to this verse or verses. Recite the verses in unison as you approach the lesson itself.

Section II—The answers to these questions are personal and should not be discussed as a group. The questions are designed to prepare each woman's heart to receive God's Word.

Section III—These questions concentrate on the actual text of God's Word. We must know what God's Word says and means before we can act upon it. Most of your study time will be spent in section III.

Section IV—As you discuss the answers to these questions, the ladies will begin to see how God's Word applies in a practical way to their lives.

Section V—Do not discuss this section. The suggestions provide a starting point for each lady to put into practice the truths of God's Word. The Holy Spirit is the One Who will bring forth fruit that will last. Close your lesson in prayer, asking God to work in each heart; or, have a brief time of silent prayer.

The effectiveness of a group Bible study usually depends on two things: (1) the leader herself; and (2) the ladies' commitment to prepare beforehand and interact during the study. You cannot totally control the second factor, but you have total control over the first one. These brief suggestions will help you be an effective Bible study leader.

You will want to prepare each lesson a week in advance. During the week, read supplemental material and look for illustrations in the everyday events of your life as well as in the lives of others.

Encourage the ladies in the Bible study to complete each lesson before the meeting itself. This preparation will make the discussion more interesting.

Also encourage the ladies to memorize the key verse or verses for each lesson. (The verse is printed in section I of each lesson.) If possible, print the verses on 3" x 5" cards to distribute each week. If you cannot do this, suggest that the ladies make their own cards and keep them in a prominent place throughout the week.

The physical setting in which you meet will have some bearing on the study itself. An informal circle of chairs, chairs around a table, someone's living room or family room—these types of settings encourage people to relax and participate. In addition to an informal setting, create an atmosphere in which ladies feel free to participate and be themselves.

During the discussion time, here are a few things to observe:

• Don't do all the talking. This is not designed to be a lecture.

• Encourage discussion on each question by adding ideas and questions.

• Don't discuss controversial issues that will divide the group. (Differences of opinion are healthy; divisions are not.)

• Don't allow one lady to dominate the discussion. Use statements such as these to draw others into the study: "Let's hear from someone on this side of the room" (the side opposite the dominant talker); "Let's hear from someone who has not shared yet today."

• Stay on the subject. The tendency toward tangents is always possible in a discussion. One of your responsibilities as the leader is to keep the group on the track.

• Don't get bogged down on a question that interests only one person.

You may want to use the last fifteen minutes of the scheduled time for prayer. If you have a large group of ladies, divide into smaller groups for prayer. You could call this the "Share and Care Time."

If you have a morning Bible study, encourage the ladies to go out for lunch with someone else from time to time. This is a good way to get acquainted with new ladies. Occasionally you could plan a time when ladies bring their own lunches or salads to share and eat together. These things help promote fellowship and friendship in the group.

The formats that follow are suggestions only. You can plan your own format, use one of these, or adapt one of these to your needs.

2-hour Bible Study

10:00—10:15 Coffee and fellowship time

10:15—10:30 Get-acquainted time
> Have two ladies take five minutes each to tell something about themselves and their families.
> Also use this time to make announcements and, if appropriate, take an offering for the babysitters.

10:30—11:45 Bible study
> Leader guides discussion of the questions in the day's lesson.

11:45—12:00 Prayer time

2-hour Bible Study

10:00—10:45 Bible lesson
> Leader teaches a lesson on the content of the material. No discussion during this time.

10:45—11:00 Coffee and fellowship

11:00—11:45 Discussion time
> Divide into small groups with an appointed leader for each group. Discuss the questions in the day's lesson.

11:45—12:00 Prayer time

1¹/₂-hour Bible Study

10:00—10:30 Bible study
> Leader guides discussion of half the questions in the day's lesson.

10:30—10:45 Coffee and fellowship

10:45—11:15 Bible study
> Leader continues discussion of the questions in the day's lesson.

11:15—11:30 Prayer time

ANSWERS FOR LEADER'S USE

Information inside parentheses ( ) is additional instruction for the group leader.

LESSON 1

Introduction (To stimulate thought: How effectively could an artist paint a portrait on a piece of canvas that was not fastened to a wooden framework?)

Section I (Recite the verses together and answer the questions.)

1. He knows them. He gives them eternal life. They are safe in His hand.

2. They hear His voice. They follow Him.

Section III—1. Under sin.

2. All have sinned.

3. Dead, trespasses, sins.

4. We don't realize we need salvation unless we first realize we have sinned against God. *(Discuss:* In what ways were you a slave to sin prior to salvation? How did salvation "free" you from sin's slavery? Do you think it is easy or hard for people to admit they are sinners? [This discussion may be a helpful testimony to unsaved ladies in your group.])

5. The ungodly.

6. While we were yet sinners.

7. Our sins.

8. Mercy.

9. Come to Christ and believe on Him.

10. Receive us, give us eternal life, raise us from death.

11. Acts 16:31 and John 1:12 are two possible references.

12. We shall be saved.

13. John 3:16—Whoever believes *will have* eternal life. John 10:27-29—Jesus' sheep will *never* perish. 1 John 5:11-13—He that has the Son *has life*; we can *know* this. Jude 24—God is able to keep us from *falling* (losing our salvation). *(Discuss:* How should the certainty of eternal life affect your life?)

14. (1) Sinned; (2) Christ, sins; (3) believe, saved; (4) perish.

Section IV (Share answers.)

LESSON 2

Introduction (To stimulate thought: Relate a time when, due to impatience, you skipped some steps while doing a task. Describe the results.)

Section I (Recite the verses together and answer the questions.)

1. As Lord.

2. A ruler of preeminence to whom service and obedience are due.

Section III—1. Psalm 119:73—God made and formed me. Psalm 139:15, 16—God has been concerned about me since conception; He has planned my days. Exodus 4:10, 11—God has made me what I am; He can work through my weakness to His glory. Proverbs 16:9—The Lord works things out according to His purposes. Proverbs 16:4—All things, good or bad, will accomplish God's plan. Romans 8:28, 29—God uses all the circumstances of our lives for our good in order to make us like His Son.

2. God made me exactly what I am, and HE can use me as I yield my life to Him. I can rest in the fact that He has a plan for me and that He

can use all circumstances for my good to accomplish His purposes.

3. Job 23:10—"tried"; I shall come forth as gold; God knows what is happening to me. Psalm 119:67—"afflicted"; I obey Thy Word; before I had trials, I went astray. Romans 5:3—"tribulation"; produces patience or endurance; rejoice! 2 Corinthians 4:17—"affliction"; it is achieving eternal glory; it is light and momentary in comparison to eternity. Hebrews 12:11—"chastening"; produces a harvest of righteousness and peace; we are exercised or trained by it, even though it may be unpleasant. 1 Peter 1:6, 7—"temptations"; they prove the genuineness of our faith and they glorify Christ; trials are only "for a season."

4. Trust in God's continued presence in trials and know that they are being used for our ultimate spiritual good. Trials are brief in light of eternity with Christ.

5. She will continue to cling to the Lord through good times and bad. She will keep progressing in holiness as He works in her. Her life of spiritual fruit will be her defense.

Section IV—1. Personal answers. *(Discuss:* If a woman reacts to these circumstances with bitterness and resentment, what will be the results in her life? Can you recall a person whose trials resulted in greater godliness and spiritual beauty in her life? What is the difference between how we *feel* during suffering and what we *know?)*

2. Share answers.

3. Pride, fear, self-centeredness, self-sufficiency, worldliness, hardheartedness.

4. Humility, dependence on God, trust, desire for God, and godliness.

5. Busyness, putting self first, yielding to materialism and humanism, physical difficulties. *(Discuss:* What happens when a woman says, "I want Christ to be my Savior, but that's it." [She will be unfruitful, ungrateful for her salvation, and ineffective; 2 Pet. 1:5-9.] How can women encourage each other to make Christ Lord of their lives? [Be a godly friend; encourage church attendance; share good books and Christ-exalting music; listen and give Biblical counsel; pray together.])

LESSON 3

Introduction (To stimulate thought: In the unbelieving world today, to what things do people look to help them make changes in their lives? [Possible answers include psychology, books, support groups, "experts," religion/cults.] Do these changes usually last? Why or why not?)

Section I (Recite the verses together and answer the questions.)

1. Wonderful; gives light.

2. Brings light to the dark areas of our lives (exposes sin); gives understanding (of salvation and Christian living).

3. He obeyed God's Word.

Section III—1. In believers.

2. He is their Comforter; He guides them into God's truth; He dwells in them; He teaches spiritual truth. *(Discuss:* What strikes you as being unique about God's plan to put His own Spirit in each believer? How do you know God's Spirit is in you? [See Romans 8:14, 16, 23, 26.])

3. The Spirit of God and the flesh (the sin principle within us).

4. "In the Spirit."

5. The Spirit tells us what to do and also gives the power to do it. It is a God-produced life, which we live by faith. (The word "walk" has the idea of ordering one's conduct. Once we are saved, we should be willing to live our lives [i.e., order our conduct] according to the Holy Spirit, Who indwells us.)

6. We will not give in to the flesh, the sin principle.

7. We do what we know we shouldn't do. We struggle with sinful habits and are controlled by sin's passions and desires.

8. Love, joy, peace, longsuffering, gentleness, goodness, faithfulness, meekness, and self-control.

9. A believer must understand that sin no longer has a right to rule over her (Rom. 6). She is spiritually alive in Christ. As she abides in Him daily, the Holy Spirit's power will enable her to put off fleshly desires and sins.

10. The flesh would run rampant in us. The Spirit's work restrains it. Romans 7:18 states, "For I know that in me (that is, in my flesh,) dwelleth no good thing."

11. Grieve the Spirit; quench the Spirit. *(Discuss:* What pictures do the words "quench" and "grieve" create in your mind? What do these words mean?)

12. By not being submissive to the Lord, not reading His Word, and not praying.

13. Me!

14. God (His Spirit; 2 Pet. 1:21).

15. Teaching/doctrine (This is the path); reproof (You're off the path); correction (This is how to get back on the path); instruction in righteousness (This is how to stay on the path).

16. To make us mature in every area of our faith; to equip us for every

good work He desires us to do. *(Discuss:* Why do you think God revealed Himself and His will to us in written form? Why is it beneficial to us?)

17. We should love it, delight in it, and find our spiritual nourishment there. *(Discuss:* What attitude do you think Christians in general have toward God's Word? Why? How do we develop love and respect for God's Word? How do we learn to delight in it?)

18. Acts 17:11—search the Scriptures daily; Psalm 119:11—hide God's Word in our hearts (memorize it); Psalm 119:97—meditate on it daily; James 1:22—do what it says.

Section IV—1. (a) Confessing sin; asking for the Spirit's filling; spending time in God's Word; being obedient to His Word; asking God to work in us; being sensitive to His Spirit's leading; resisting Satan's attacks through Christ's blood and God's Word. (b) God will be able to work in you and through you.

2. So that we will be wise unto salvation; in order to live lives that please God.

3. Possible answers include godliness, peace, faith. (See the following verses for the qualities of a person who values God's Word: Joshua 1:8; Psalms 19:7, 8; 119:38, 50, 98-100, 165.)

4. Personal answers.

LESSON 4

Introduction (To stimulate thought: Ask group members to name people in the Bible who illustrate the fact that sinful thoughts lead to sinful words and actions. Possible answers include Cain, Saul, David, Judas, Ananias and Sapphira.)

Section I (Recite the verse together and answer the questions.)

1. Her mind is occupied with what the flesh desires; e.g., self, pleasure, money, reputation.

2. She is thinking about the Lord and what the Spirit prompts her to do through God's Word.

Section III—1. The Lord searches and examines our hearts and minds.

2. Matthew 15:16-20—evil thoughts; Romans 1:28-31—wickedness, evil, greed, depravity; Philippians 3:18, 19—earthly things.

3. 1 Samuel 12:24—what great things God has done for us; Psalm 63:6—God Himself; Psalm 77:11, 12—God's works and mighty deeds of the past; Psalm 107:43—God's loving-kindness; Psalm 119:15, 99, 148—God's precepts, ways, testimonies, and word; Philippians 4:8—things that are true, honest, just, pure, lovely, of good report; Hebrews

3:1—the Lord Jesus; Hebrews 10:24—how we can encourage others to do good.

4. Romans 12:2—Renew our minds by focusing on God's will and not being conformed to the world. Colossians 3:16—Let God's Word dwell in us abundantly. Hebrews 4:12—Let God's Word judge our thoughts and attitudes. Psalm 119:11—Memorize Scripture. Joshua 1:8—Meditate on God's Word throughout the day and determine to obey it. 2 Corinthians 10:5—Make our thoughts obedient to Christ. Philippians 4:6, 7—Worry about nothing and pray about everything. Hebrews 4:16—Ask God for help in this area.

5. Isaiah 26:3—peace; Romans 8:6—life and peace; Philippians 4:6, 7—peace.

6. Matthew 22:37—We are to love God with our minds. Our love for God is not founded on what we feel but on the work of the Spirit in our souls, the decisions of our minds, and the commitment and obedience of our wills. 1 Corinthians 2:14-16—As believers, we have the mind of Christ. This enables us to have spiritual insight into God's Word. This is not true of the unsaved person. The believer's mind has been redeemed!

Section IV—1. Many Christians probably give no conscious thought to the fact that God is judging their thoughts. Knowing God is judging our thoughts should cause us to judge them first and seek to make our thought-life pleasing to God. Immoral thoughts, worry, self-centered thoughts, thoughts of revenge or evil toward someone—these are sin and need to be dealt with by confessing and forsaking them. *(Discuss: What usually happens when a Christian is more concerned about what others see outwardly than on the spiritual condition of her heart and mind?)*

2. Personal answers. *(Discuss:* What kinds of thoughts keep us from thinking about the Lord and spiritual things? Discuss the kinds of activities and habits that reinforce ungodly thoughts; e.g., immoral, unethical TV shows; worldly music; humanistic and ungodly magazines and books; gossip; worry; preoccupation with material things; fantasizing.)

3. Personal answers. *(Discuss:* What activities or resources help you think about God and His Word? Possible answers include consistent church attendance, Bible study, prayer, Christ-exalting music, reliable Christian reading materials, Scripture memorization.)

4. Personal answers.

5. (a) The opposite of a Spirit-controlled mind is a sinful mind, and sin is characterized by unrest. Also, peace is an evidence of the Spirit's

work in our lives (Gal. 5:22). (b) The sin-filled mind experiences the unrest that is characteristic of sin (Isa. 48:22; 57:21).

6. Personal answers.

LESSON 5

Introduction (To stimulate thought: Before you were saved, did you feel guilty if you had a bad attitude about someone or something? If so, did you try to change it? Since you have been saved, are you bothered by bad attitudes? Why do you think this is?

Section I (Recite the verses together and answer the questions.)

1. The old, sinful nature that controlled us before we were saved.
2. Righteousness and true holiness.
3. Put off the old man and put on the new man.

Section III—1. Genesis 13:1-17—Abram (Abraham) let his nephew Lot go first in choosing the part of the land in which he would dwell. Lot chose a better portion of land, but he dwelled near the wicked city of Sodom. God gave Abram even more land and confirmed His covenant to Abram again. Genesis 45:1-15—Joseph revealed himself to his brothers, who had sold him to slave-traders many years before. Rather than being harsh and bitter, he showed loving concern for his brothers and assured them that everything had happened according to God's plan. 1 Samuel 24:1-15—Saul was trying to find David, his successor to the throne of Israel, to kill him. David had an opportunity to kill Saul instead, but he did not. David displayed respect for the man whom God had appointed to be Israel's first king. 1 Samuel 25:2-35—When David's men asked wealthy Nabal for supplies, he refused to grant their request. David went to kill Nabal. Abigail, Nabal's wife, intervened. She humbly asked David to reconsider his actions and to forgive her for her husband's actions. David eventually thanked Abigail for keeping him from killing Nabal. Acts 15:36-41—John Mark had left Paul and Barnabas in the midst of the first missionary journey (Acts 13:13). Barnabas was willing to put the incident in the past and use John Mark again. Paul was not. Barnabas lived up to his name, "son of encouragement" (Acts 4:36), and took Barnabas with him. (John Mark was evidently "rehabilitated" by Barnabas. Later Paul described him as "profitable to me for the ministry" [2 Tim. 4:11].)

2. Christ abased Himself; He didn't grasp at His equality with God the Father; He was willing to become a servant of God and man; He was willing to endure suffering; He was humble.

3. Luke 5:12, 13—Jesus touched a leper, the outcast in Biblical times. *(Discuss:* What is our attitude toward today's "outcasts"; e.g., people with AIDS, homosexuals, prostitutes? Are we willing to reach out and

touch them?) Luke 19:1-10—Jesus was willing to associate with sinners because He knew they were lost and needed a Savior. Mark 10:13-16—Jesus showed tenderness to little children; He took time for them. John 8:1-11—Jesus loved the woman taken in adultery; He was sensitive to her feelings and needs. John 13:4, 5—Jesus displayed humility and servanthood when He washed the disciples' feet.

4. Possible answers include unconditional love, preferring others, spiritual zeal, willingness to share and show hospitality, seeking harmony with others, sharing joy and pain with others, humility, honesty, peace.

5. The conviction of the Spirit through God's Word (vv. 12, 13); the fact that God knows our attitudes (v. 12); the fact that Jesus knows our weaknesses (v. 15); the invitation to come boldly to God's throne to obtain mercy and grace (v. 16).

Section IV—1. Some thoughts that help us deal with wrong attitudes are: (1) considering others better than ourselves; (2) centering our thoughts on the greatness of God and the finiteness of man (pride causes criticism; humility brings God's grace to us [James 4:6]); (3) thinking of Christ, Who did not become bitter when misunderstood and falsely accused. *(Discuss:* How do we know when someone has a bad attitude about something? [Sarcasm, complaining, criticism, anger, defensiveness, self-justification, blame-shifting.] If it is our place to do so, how can we lovingly help someone who has a bad attitude?)

2. Personal answers.

3. Ideas include continual feeding on God's Word; realizing that God sees my bad attitudes; not excusing bad attitudes, but confessing them as evidence of the sin in me; asking God to show me attitudes of which I am not aware; picturing my secret thoughts and attitudes as exposed for all to see.

LESSON 6

Introduction (To stimulate thought: Ask your group to give examples of hurtful speech and helpful speech.)

Section I (Recite the verse together and answer the questions.)

1. Lying, gossip, faultfinding, backbiting, harsh criticism, slander, profanity.

2. Good, edifying, ministering grace.

Section III—1. Eve—Eve's conversation with Satan led to her disobedience of God's command. Rebekah—Rebekah talked Jacob into deceiving his father, Isaac. Potiphar's wife—She tried to entice Joseph with her words. Then she lied about him, and he was imprisoned as a result. Delilah—Delilah nagged Samson daily (v. 16) until he finally gave in and revealed the source of his strength. Sapphira—She lied, just as her husband had done; she died immediately.

2. Deborah—She used wise words as a judge in Israel and to encourage Barak to fight the enemy; later, she raised her voice in praise. Ruth—Ruth used beautiful words to affirm her love for her mother-in-law, Naomi, and Naomi's God. Esther—Esther used brave words to inform the king of Haman's evil plot against her people, the Jews. Samaritan woman—The woman at the well used her words to convince the men of Sychar to listen to the words of Christ. Priscilla—Priscilla, with her husband, Aquila, helped Apollos understand spiritual truth.

3. If a woman can control her tongue, she is probably also working on her thoughts, attitudes, and actions. She is maturing spiritually.

4. Offends, boasts, corrupts, curses men, is hypocritical, denies the truth, fights and quarrels, speaks evil. Attitudes include pride, anger, bitterness, selfishness, worldliness, critical spirit, self-sufficiency.

5. James knew believers had many problems with their words. He wanted them to realize their ungodliness in this area.

6. To show us how we sin with our lips. It is an area of continual challenge. The Lord wants us to be holy in all areas. *(Discuss:* Have things changed much since James wrote his letter? What "speech problems" do we have in churches today?)

7. Lying, angry words, unwholesome words, brawling words, slander, obscenity, foolish talk, coarse joking, empty (vain) words, unwise speech.

8. Truthful, helpful, building up, kind, compassionate, loving, pure, thankful, wise, speaking and singing spiritual encouragement, humble. (Note that in Ephesians Paul gives "therapy" for speech problems. To counteract falsehood, speak the truth. To correct unwholesome talk, replace it with helpful, edifying speech. In place of brawling and slander, use kind, compassionate words.)

9. We are to put off the words of the old, sinful nature, such as gossip, indecent talk, boasting, lying, and angry words. Because we are being transformed in our attitudes, we are to put on speech that reflects our new life: loving, edifying, patient, truthful, thankful, and rejoicing words.

Section IV—1. Personal answers.

2. Obeying Paul's commands will lead to harmony within a church or family or among friends. We may not always agree with one another, but we can learn to speak kindly to each other.

3. Personal answers.

LESSON 7

Introduction (To stimulate thought: Do you agree or disagree with this statement: Actions speak louder than words? Explain your answer.)

    Section 1—(Recite the verse together and answer the questions.)

    1. Having a right relationship with God and man.

    2. Primarily through God's Word and the conviction of the Holy Spirit.

    3. No. James asserts that we all stumble in many ways (James 3:2). In the original language, the idea of 1 John 3:9 ("whosoever is born of God doth not commit sin") is that a born-again person does not continue to keep on in her sin. A true child of God will show some conviction of sin and growth in holiness.

    4. Doing right; loving her fellow-believer.

    Section III—1. John 8:29—He did things that please God. John 13:2-5—He served others. John 14:31—He obeyed the Father's commandment. Acts 10:38—He did good through the Holy Spirit's power in Him. John 17:4—He glorified God; He completed His work. John 19:25-27—He cared for the needs of others despite His own suffering. 1 Peter 2:23—He did not retaliate mistreatment.

    2. Adultery, fornication, uncleanness (impurity), lasciviousness (lustful, lewd deeds), idolatry, witchcraft, hatred, variance (discord), emulations (envious ambitions), wrath, strife, seditions (dissension), heresies, envyings, murders, drunkenness, revellings (wild parties, carousing).

    3. Producing fruit takes time and cultivation as the Spirit works in us. Fruit is a product of maturity. It is desirable, nurturing. The word creates a mental image of the Vine and the branches and the necessity of abiding in Christ to bring forth fruit (John 15), rather than producing it in our own strength.

    4. Both passages express the idea that a person may say she is a child of God, but her acts may deny it; love is singled out as being of primary importance.

    5. We will not harm our neighbor; we will not do the works of darkness; we will not behave indecently; we will not act with strife or jealousy; we will not fulfill the desires of the sinful nature.

    6. Love thy neighbor as thyself; cast off the works of darkness; put on the armor of light; walk (behave) honestly; put on the Lord Jesus Christ; do not make provision for fulfilling the lusts of the flesh.

    7. Love (vv. 8-10); the return of Christ (vv. 11, 12). *(Discuss:* How do these two factors motivate you to act righteously?)

Section IV—1. Impurity may be in the thought-life as well as in open actions; idolatry occurs in the heart; hatred or jealousy may be hidden, but each will surface sooner or later; someone who has selfish ambition in her heart may appear to other people to be simply a hard worker. *(Discuss*: Do Christians, in general, consider acts such as jealousy, envy, selfish ambition, promoting discord, and dissension as terrible as the other sins in the Galatians 5 list? Explain. Do you think New Testament believers struggled more with these vices than we do today?)

2. Examples: An attitude of faithfulness will cause me to go to church when I feel like staying home; an attitude of kindness will prevent me from being harsh with my children; an attitude of goodness will prompt me to do a good deed for someone whose personality may irritate me; an attitude of self-control will enable me to serve my husband when I don't feel like it.

3. YOU: Works of the flesh create problems of all sorts and destroy peace; OTHERS: Works of the flesh hurt others; in some cases, I would be using people; TESTIMONY: Works of the flesh nullify my witness for Christ; they do not attract the unsaved.

4. YOU: The fruit of the Spirit reduces problems, friction, and worry; it increases joy; OTHERS: The fruit of the Spirit shows people they are valuable to me and to God; TESTIMONY: People would want to know what makes such a difference in my life.

5. Love: Jesus ministered to Mary and Martha in their time of grief (John 11:1-46); joy: the salvation of the lost brings joy to the heart of Christ (John 4:31-36); peace: Jesus slept in the midst of the storm (Mark 4:35-38); long-suffering: He explained again and again to His disciples Who He was and what He had come to do (e.g., John 14:9); gentleness: He took time and care with little children (Mark 10:13-16); goodness: all of Christ's ministry to people was evidence of His goodness; faith: He trusted the Father's will (Matt. 26:36-46); meekness: He submitted to suffering—even though He could have been delivered by angels (Matt. 26:47-56); self-control—He resisted Satan's temptations (Matt. 4:1-11). *(Discuss:* What actions specifically demonstrate love and concern for others? Answers include hugs, appropriate touches, smiles, eye contact, paying attention, listening without interrupting, serving, intercessory prayer, telephone calls, written notes.)

LESSON 8
Introduction (To stimulate thought: Ask members of your group to recall good deeds done by them or to them that obviously came from a heart of love for the Lord.)

Section I (Recite the verse together and answer the questions.)

1. Jesus was sitting on a mountain when He spoke the words of Matthew 5. The multitudes may have been within hearing range of Him.

2. His disciples.

3. To let other people see the outworking of our faith in God and love for Him in all areas of life.

Section III—1. Proverbs 31:20—helping the poor and needy; Luke 10:33, 34—helping people with physical needs; Acts 9:36, 39—using one's abilities and resources to help others; Romans 12:13—sharing; showing hospitality; 2 Corinthians 1:10, 11—praying for others; Galatians 6:2—helping others bear their burdens; 1 Timothy 5:9, 10—raising children; showing hospitality; serving; helping those in need; 1 Timothy 6:17-19—sharing one's material blessings with others; James 1:27—looking after children in need and widows in distress.

2. John 15:4, 5—abiding in Christ; Romans 12:6-8—using our spiritual gifts; 2 Corinthians 9:8—God's grace; Galatians 5:22, 23—the fruit of the Spirit; Ephesians 2:8-10—God's salvation and work in me; Ephesians 4:11, 12—the ministry of the gifted men who lead the church; 2 Thessalonians 1:11—prayer and God's power; 2 Timothy 2:20, 21—cleansing from sin; 2 Timothy 3:16, 17—knowledge of the Scriptures; James 3:17—wisdom from above.

3. Matthew 5:16—to bring glory to Himself; Ephesians 4:11-13—to build up, edify, and unify the church; 1 Timothy 2:9, 10—to demonstrate godliness; James 2:17, 18—to demonstrate that our faith is genuine; 1 Peter 2:12—to put unbelievers to shame; to cause them to acknowledge God; 1 Peter 4:10—to serve others and administer God's grace.

4. Luke 10:25-37—mercy, concern, no thought of self or inconvenience; Acts 2:42-47—the advancing of the cause of Christ and the desire to help fellow believers; Acts 4:32-37—unity; desire to share; Philippians 2:3-7—humility; self-sacrifice; desire to be like Christ; James 3:13—humility; wisdom; 1 John 3:16-18; 5:2— love for God and others.

Section IV—1. Abiding in Christ ("For without me ye can do nothing").

2. Love for the Lord; obedience to God; concern for the welfare of others.

3. Possible answers include trying to gain favor with God, trying to look spiritual rather than being spiritual, pride. *(Discuss:* Name a person or people in the Bible who did something that seemed spiritual but with the wrong motives or attitudes. Examples include Cain [Gen. 4:1-15]; King Saul [1 Sam. 15:1-28]; the Pharisees [Matt. 23:1-28];

Ananias and Sapphira [Acts 5:1-11]). What was the result in every case? [Rejection by God.])

4. Personal answers. *(Discuss:* Do Christians today live up to this standard? Why or why not?)

5. By asking God to show us what He has ordained, or prepared, for us to do that day (Eph. 2:10).

6. Personal answers.

LESSON 9

Introduction (To stimulate thought: What values of society today influence our outward appearance? [We are told we must look young, thin, rich, successful, sexy, self-confident, poised.] How are we bombarded with these messages? (TV, magazines, stores, catalogs, our peers.])

Section I (Recite the verses together and answer the questions.)

1. No. Our primary concern must be on developing inner spiritual beauty above outward beauty.

2. A meek and quiet spirit.

Section III—1. Genesis 4:4, 5—Cain's anger was reflected in his face. Nehemiah 2:1, 2—Nehemiah's sadness of heart showed on his face. Proverbs 7:10, 13—A brazen face reflects an immoral heart. Ecclesiastes 8:1—True wisdom will brighten the face. Isaiah 3:8, 9— Rebelliousness and wickedness are displayed in one's countenance. Daniel 7:28—Being troubled in spirit is reflected on the face.

2. Proverbs 15:13—cheerful; Proverbs 15:30—smiling ("light of the eyes" is literally "bright eyes" or "cheerful look"); Psalm 34:4, 5—radiant, free from anxiety; 2 Corinthians 3:18—reflecting the Lord's glory.

3. Our faces are visual monitors of what is going on in our hearts. In general, cheerfulness, peace, and trust will be seen on our faces as we walk in a loving, vital relationship with our heavenly Father.

4. God created two distinct sexes, and He desires a clear differentiation between them. Unisex is out!

5. Modesty (not attracting attention); shamefacedness (decency; conforming to standards of taste and morality); sobriety (propriety; not offending the rules between the sexes; appropriate); discretion (cautious, reserved, showing good judgment).

6. Matthew 6:28-33—Unsaved people make this a focal point of life. Our hearts should be set on things above. Worry shows a lack of trust in God to provide for our needs. God is not against beauty—just look at His creation! Isaiah 3:16-24—They were proud and lacked discretion and modesty. They were ostentatious in their dress. They gave no thought to God or their spiritual condition, and they were self-

centered. 1 Corinthians 6:19, 20—Since my body is the temple of God and He owns it, it should reflect in every way His character (holiness, purity, order, etc.).

Section IV—1. Get adequate sleep, relaxation, and fresh air. Eat right and exercise. Wear your best colors to highlight your eyes and smile. Take time to groom properly. Have humor in your life and smile more! Take time for God.

2. By the use of feminine colors, fabrics, and styles in clothing; delicate, modest accent pieces; soft fragrances. Avoid the "hard" look in clothes, hairstyles, and makeup.

3. Personal answers.

4. I should look like a woman who belongs to God. I should not wear an outfit (jewelry, hairstyle, etc.) that will attract improper attention to myself. (Remember, it's better to over-cover than over-expose!)

LESSON 10

Introduction (To stimulate thought: Have a brief brainstorming session, listing some problems we face with regard to time; e.g., too much to do, too little to do, needing adequate family time, finding quiet time, organizing our time.)

Section I (Recite the verses together and answer the questions.)

1. Foolish and wise.

2. Circumspectly (carefully), wisely, redeeming the time, understanding God's will.

Section III—1. 1 Chronicles 29:15—a shadow; Psalm 39:5—a handbreadth ($2^{1}/_{2}$ to 4 inches); Psalm 102:11—a declining shadow and withering grass; James 4:4—a vapor or mist.

2. Luke 12:16-21—The rich man's time was spent thinking about and planning material things and hedonistic pleasure. He was totally self-consumed. He took no thought of God and did not consider that He is in control of time and life spans. Luke 12:42-47—The steward lost his sense of responsibility. Time became a commodity to be used for his own ends. James 4:13-16—This man boasts as if he is in control of the days of his life and his circumstances. He also gives no thought to the Lord.

3. 2 Thessalonians 3:11, 12—Don't be idle; spend time doing constructive things. 1 Timothy 5:13, 14—Avoid spending time being a busybody and gossip. Proverbs 6:6-11—Don't be lazy, but industrious. Work now for what will happen in the future. Proverbs 12:24, 27—Laziness puts one in bondage to others and causes great waste of resources. Diligence leads to the right kind of self-sufficiency and resourcefulness.

4. Mark 6:30, 31—sharing with others what the Lord has done; eating; resting; Mark 6:45, 46—praying; Luke 18:15-17—taking time to minister to children; John 4:4-30—sharing the gospel; Acts 17:11—searching the Scriptures; Psalm 119:97—thinking about God's Word; 1 Thessalonians 4:11—working; 1 Timothy 5:9, 10, 14—caring for the home and children; doing good deeds; showing hospitality; Titus 2:3-5—teaching; meeting family needs; showing kindness; helping others; Hebrews 10:25—assembling together with other believers; encouraging others.

5. Ruth—She made the most of the opportunity to work for food. She worked hard and steadily. She took rest when needed. The virtuous woman—She utilizes daily time wisely, not wastefully. She cares for the needs of her family. She completes her work. She keeps future developments in view and prepares to meet them. Dorcas—She spent time doing good and helping the needy. She was not self-centered in her use of time. Women Paul knew—They worked hard for the Lord and for His church.

6. Psalm 90:12—Keep in mind the brevity of life and the value of time. James 1:5—Ask God for wisdom to know how to use time. Psalm 119:169, 170—Pray about God's will for our lives and read His Word to help us know it. Proverbs 19:20—Get counsel from other people on priorities and time management.

Section IV—1. Not in idleness, laziness, wastefulness, self-centeredness, pleasure seeking, or being a busybody.

2. Possible answers include husband, parents, grandparents, friends, older women, godly teachers. Also, books are helpful.

3. Personal answers.

LESSON 11

Introduction (To stimulate thought: The Bible presents many case studies on relationships. Name some Biblical relationships that were a source of blessing to the people involved. [Possible answers: David and Jonathan—1 Sam. 18:1-4; Jesus and Mary, Martha, and Lazarus—Luke 10:38-42 and John 11:1-46; Paul and Timothy—Acts 16:1-3 and 2 Tim. 1:1, 2; Aquila, Priscilla, and Apollos—Acts 18:24-26.])

Section I (Recite the verse together and answer the questions.)

1. All people, believers (the household of faith).

2. Do good!

Section III—1. 1 Corinthians 9:19-23—Find a common factor with people in order to open doors for sharing the gospel with them. *(Discuss:* Is Paul saying that we may have to act like sinners in order

to win them to Christ? How might Christians misuse this verse?)
Colossians 4:5, 6—Be wise in your actions toward them. Be careful in
your speech; let it be gracious. Be aware of opportunities to tactfully
witness to them. Titus 3:1, 2—Be a good citizen so no one can fault
you. Speak no word of slander. Be peaceable, considerate, and meek.
Hebrews 12:14—Live in harmony and holiness.

2. Verse 27—love, do good; verse 28—bless, pray for; verse 30—
give; verse 31—do to them as you would like done to you; verse 35—
love, do good, lend; verse 36—be merciful.

3. Romans 15:5-7—likeminded; Ephesians 5:21—submit; Ephesians
6:18—pray; Colossians 3:12-14—forbear (bear with), forgive, love;
Colossians 3:16—teach, admonish; 1 Thessalonians 5:14, 15—warn,
comfort, support, be patient; James 1:19—listen, be slow to speak,
slow to anger; 1 Peter 4:8-10—love, show hospitality, serve. *(Discuss:*
Why is hospitality important in our relationship with other believers?)

Section IV—1. Our lives may be the only "Bible" some people will
read. We may help or hinder their salvation.

2. Tactful, gracious speech should put them at ease with us. (At
times an unbeliever will react negatively due to the Spirit's conviction.
It should never be due to rudeness on our part!) Humility should keep
us from an air of pride and self-righteousness. Seeing common factors
will give us stepping-stones to a better relationship, rather than
focusing on the huge gap that exists in the spiritual realm.

3. Personal answers.

4. Personal answers. *(Discuss:* How can we deal with the pain of
difficult relationships?)

5. Luke recorded that Jesus "went about doing good" (Acts 10:38).
Jesus wept over the city of the Jerusalem and expressed His love for
the city (Luke 19:41; Matt. 23:37-39). The ultimate demonstration of
His love was His death on the cross for sinners (Rom. 5:8). While on
the cross, He asked His Father to forgive His persecutors (Luke 23:34).

6. Love demonstrates that we are Christ's disciples. The condition
and effective work of the Church depend upon unity and love among
believers.

7. Personal answers.

LESSON 12

Introduction (To stimulate thought: Ask each lady to think of
someone who truly loves her. *(Discuss:* How do you know that person
really loves you?)

Section I (Recite the verses together and answer the questions.)

1. Love is the source that enables us to put all these virtues into action. The more we are aware of God's love for us, the more we will display these virtues to others.

2. Being chosen by God; receiving His holiness; recognizing God's love and forgiveness.

Section III—1. Verse 7—Love comes from God. Verse 8—God is love. Verses 9, 10—God showed His love for us by giving His Son, Whom He loved, to die for us and provide salvation. He did this for us even though we did not love Him. Verse 19—God loved first; we responded to that love. *(Discuss:* How do God's actions toward us—past, present, and future—reveal His love for us?)

2. Verses 7, 11, 21—We love others. Verse 16—We live in close relationship with Him. Verses 17, 18—We do not fear judgment or God's wrath; love becomes the motivation for godly living. Verse 5:3—We obey His commands.

3. Verse 12—Our love for others is an indication of our relationship to God. Verse 20—The extent of our love for fellow believers is an indication of how much we love God. Verse 5:2—If we love God and obey His commands, we will love others.

4. Love is the factor that gives true meaning to our use of spiritual gifts. A lack of love nullifies the most impressive deed. Love erases pride.

5. Possible answers (but certainly others are equally valid): thoughts—envies not, thinks no evil, believes the best, hopes the best; attitudes—vaunteth not itself, is not puffed up, seeks not her own, is not easily provoked, rejoices in the truth, rejoices not in evil, bears all things, endures all things; words—is kind, vaunteth not itself; actions—suffers long, is kind, does not behave unseemly.

6. Love keeps going even when others things fail or cease to exist.

7. Faith, in Heaven, will become sight. Hope will be fulfilled. Love will go on forever and forever.

Section IV—1. Personal answers.

2. Possible answers include guilt, a poor relationship with an earthly father, ignorance of the Scriptures, a "works versus grace" mind-set.

3. Study the Scriptures that reflect God's great love toward us; remember how God cared for us in the past; not build walls between us and God (i.e., keep sin confessed and our hearts soft toward Him).

4. Possible answers include read and study the Bible, think about Him, sing hymns and listen to God-glorifying music, express our gratitude in prayer.

5. Realize that I am a sinner and He loves me, so I should love others the same way. He said, "Love one another." If I want to please Him, I must obey his commands. It will be His continual work in me to enable me to love others in all the areas of my life. (*Discuss:* What are some attitudes that hinder us from loving others?)

6. Personal answers.

7. Personal answers.

LESSON 13

Introduction (To stimulate thought: What people in the Bible come to mind with regard to the word "prayer"? [e.g., Hannah—1 Sam 1, 2; Daniel—Dan. 6; Paul—Phil. 1:4.] What people do you associate with the word "praise"? [e.g., David—Ps. 103; Mary—Luke 1; Paul—Phil. 1:3.])

Section I (Recite the verse together and answer the questions.)

1. She praised the Lord for Who He is and what He had done for her.

2. God.

Section III—1. Matthew 6:9—worship, praise; Matthew 6:10—God's will to be done and our yielding to it; Matthew 6:11—petition for daily needs; Matthew 6:12—confession of sin; Matthew 6:13—deliverance from temptation; Matthew 5:43, 44—our enemies; Matthew 9:38—workers to go and to win people to Christ. (*Discuss:* Why did the Lord Jesus, Who is God, need to pray?)

2. Ephesians 6:18—other believers; Philippians 4:6—prayer and thanks for everything; 1 Thessalonians 5:17, 18—all situations, including giving thanks for all things; 1 Timothy 2:1, 2—all people, including government officials. (*Discuss:* What kind of prayer life did the apostle Paul have? See references such as Ephesians 1:15-17; 3:14-21; Philippians 1:3-5; 1 Thessalonians 1:2, 3; 2 Timothy 1:3.)

3. Revelation 5:11, 12—He is worthy of it. Romans 1:20, 21—It keeps us from turning away from Him and becoming foolish and proud in our thoughts. 1 Peter 2:9—It is our calling and privilege. 1 Thessalonians 5:18—It is God's will. Psalm 95:1-7—He is a great God; He made all things and people; He cares for us. Psalm 71:14-18—We declare His attributes, His salvation, and His mighty acts; we tell the next generation about God and His power. (*Discuss:* Why is it important to tell the next generation of God's glory? What will happen if we are silent?)

4. It promoted unity. The believers knew each other's needs and could help meet them. It produced fellowship and joy. It was a mutual encouragement as they walked with God. They were a testimony to all people, and many were saved.

5. She brought her needs and problems to the Lord. She trusted Him to work out the results. She gave glory to God by telling others of her answered prayer.

6. She told Eli (and probably others) of God's answer to her prayer. She gave her son a name that testified of her answered prayer. ("Samuel" suggests "heard of God.") She prayed her praise to God, and it was recorded in God's Word for us to read.

7. God Himself, God's salvation, God's person, God's actions. (Other answers are possible.)

Section IV—1. Personal answers.

2. Reading the Psalms will help develop a "praise vocabulary." Begin by praising God in private prayer as Hannah did. Express praise to God in front of your children. Sing hymns of praise at home.

3. We can pray for our churches to be purified, unified, and Spirit-filled. Sincere, united prayer strengthens our faith and worship, as well as allows God's mighty power to work among us. Sharing our answers to prayer encourages others to trust God for answered prayer.

4. Personal answers.

Praise - Patty's hives nearly gone
Prayer - Carol Twiliger, Carol Oberlitner,
   Suzanne & Kyle, Gar, Tara, Jason,
   Fisher girls, Tyler Sheldon's situation
Kurt (Carol's son-in-law)

1-31-2012
Abbi's family & Mom (salvation)
Don Schafer
My attitude

2-21-2012
   Agnes - God's will
   Eloise - health issue
   Dee - eye surgery
   Vi's daughter Judy - Satan's attack

3-13-2012
   Agnes
   June
   Nancy's son Nathan
   Slav
   Eloise
Carol praise for God's provision
Pastor Bob & Sandy
Vi & Tony - absence

7-10-2012
Abby -
Nancy Patterson & family - heath & comfort
Brenda - Vi's friend
Phil & Ruth - guidance

Bold is deciding to say something when it
would be easier to say nothing.
Bold is taking advantage of opportunities
that present themselves
Bold is creating opportunities

10-18th
Tara & family
Eloise-Shealing
Mary Ann - (Carol cleans for)
Carol Oberlitner - God's will
Nancy Litweiler
Protection from deer & turkey

Tara's children

Carol's blessing little Miriam in Kenya
neighbor lost her husband

Vi's back - healing

Dorothy Shafer - heart attack
Nancy Crites - blood clot
Barb - bronchitis & blood pressure
Carol D's niece 3 yrs old tonsilitis
surgery Wednesday
Lillian - tests at Mayo
Nancy Litwiller at Mayo

Vi's children - church Easter & Mother's Day
Carol J's children to church

Angie's defense meeting
Carol's girls "Fisher" 10:00 Am Wed

Edna May - Mary's mom

Dorothy Shafer - healing

Pastor Bob
Sandy - new job   Roberta Miller
Doug - Vi's son surgery   Darrin Martin
                                   Johnahon, Sarah
Jennifer & baby   Daniel
June Beebe   VBS   Mission trip
                                   Emily
                                   Ken & Barbara